DISCARD

St. Helena Library
1492 Library Lane
St. Helena, CA 94574
(707) 963-5244

A Gift From
ST. HELENA PUBLIC LIBRARY
FRIENDS & FOUNDATION

HOME MADE BEAUTIFUL

A Guide to Incorporating Cozy Farmhouse, French Elegance, & Kentucky Charm

Kimberly Stevens Patton

COPYRIGHT NOTICE

Copyright © 2021 by Kimberly Stevens Patton

ISBN 978-1-09839-788-3

All rights reserved. This book or any portion thereof may not be reproduced or used in any manner whatsoever without the express written permission of the publisher except for the use of brief quotations in a book review.

Cover photo and some photos throughout book by Sarah Nichole Photography

Kimberly Stevens Patton
AUTHOR | DESIGNER

For my girls, Jessi and Holli. I hope you always think of me when you see a beautiful room in a home filled with love.

And for my grandmothers, aunts, sister, and mom. Thanks to you my kitchen is clean and my beds are made.

TABLE OF CONTENTS

01
Developing Your
Personal Style 1

02
Cozy Farmhouse,
French Elegance,
Kentucky Charm 9

03
Blending The Old and
the New 14

04
Building Your Nest 16

05
Flea Markets: A Designer's Favorite Pastime 24

06
Design Tips: Room By Room 32

07
Cultivating Your Outdoor Space 45

08
Holidays And Parties 55

09
Parties Throughout the Year............................90

welcome

Since I retired ten years ago, I have become a homebody. It's not in my nature to be a recluse, but I find myself most happy when puttering around inside our home.

I have always said, your home is a reflection of who you are. It doesn't matter how far you travel; your home is the safe place where you return, relax, and feed your soul. In some ways, that's what makes it home — the familiarity.

I was raised in the small town of Olive Hill Kentucky, located in the foothills of Appalachia. At home, my parents would entertain family in the afternoon on the front porch. Coffee and dessert were expected and provided. As the adults talked, we kids would play in the yard, catching lightning bugs, playing tag, and hide and go seek until everyone went home for the night.

When I decided to write this book, I wanted to share what the strong women in my life taught me about making a home beautiful. They taught me that designing a cozy, warm, and welcoming home is essential. They taught me that a home is the place where family gathers for love, laughter, and support. That design isn't about perfection. It's about comfort and fun. They taught me a lot more too, about being courteous to others, and always offering a warm welcome.

Family was always at the center of our lives, and we were extremely close. We didn't have much, but what we had, we shared, and other neighbor families returned the favor. My dad raised a couple of gardens each summer, and we always shared the rewards of his efforts with the community. When beans, tomatoes, and corn were ready to harvest, Mom or one of her sisters would be on the phone, spreading the word that it was time for canning. The women in our family would gather together in a large circle under a big shade tree and string beans or cut corn off the cob to prepare it for canning and freezing. My aunt Gertie was instrumental in the effort.

What a wonderful time we had growing up. It was the 1960s, and our little town was booming. There was plenty of work at the brickyard. We had two sewing factories where women worked, and there were two or three clothing and shoe stores where the locals shopped.

Every back yard had a clothesline, and the neighbor ladies would chat while hanging the freshly washed bed sheets and clothes out to dry. My dad made our clothesline out of some old plumbing pipe left over from one of his jobs. As far as I know, it is still there.

Growing up in Olive Hill, I learned that fine people love their families, make their home homey, and do good in the community. As I grew older, built my own family, and created my own home, I developed a style and a sense of home that blends the shadows of the past with the memories of my own children, playing throughout the house, sitting on the front porch drinking iced tea, and cultivating a garden to share.

When I sat down to begin work on this book, I started to write about the tips, tricks, and lessons I have learned over years of making a beautiful home. But as I wrote, I realized that each lesson held a memory, each trick was passed from a great designer and homemaker before me. Every space in my home, carefully created to evoke a feeling of comfort, joy, elegance, and nostalgia, is done through the weaving of design and memory together.

Throughout my home, I have created "vignettes." In the design world, this means small, pleasing groupings of objects that create snapshots of a feeling, memory, or aesthetic. But the word vignette has another meaning. It is used to describe a brief narrative illustration of a person, a place, a mood, or a time. As I started writing my notes about designing a beautiful home, these vignettes of another kind came out onto the page. They were snippets of a life well-lived and well-integrated into who I am as a designer, a mother, a daughter, a wife, and a human being.

So, throughout this book, I offer my insight into designing a beautiful home, with a Kentucky-raised, French-inspired, elegant, eclectic twist. But I also offer my memories, my thoughts, and my lessons learned.

I hope you find something within these pages that gives you a great idea to incorporate into your own home. Perhaps on a rainy day, you'll find yourself curled up in your favorite spot with your grandmother's quilt, along with this book. I hope you enjoy it.

— *Kimberly*

My first interior design project - my bedroom in '78

DEVELOPING YOUR PERSONAL STYLE.

People often ask me, "What's In?" I think they mean, what's trendy this year? Or, what should I be doing in my home to make it more attractive to guests? Or, more fearfully, what is "out" and should be removed from my home to avoid embarrassment?

The truth is, what's in for me isn't what's in for everyone. You have to be happy in your surroundings. Each home should be filled with colors, textures, and objects that bring comfort to its occupants, sparks joy, or invites a great memory.

Find what feels good to you by browsing home decor magazines, Pinterest, or home renovation TV shows. I highly recommend Architectural Digest. Find what colors feel good to you when you are flipping through magazines. Tear out the pages that catch your eye. While on vacation, study the hotel where you're staying. Look around and take in as much of the designed surroundings as you can. Take photos and make notes about what you like. Notice light, furniture, carpet, and a room's feeling.

"Beautiful tablescapes and dining outdoors can bring so much enjoyment to you and your guests."

Add this information to your repertoire, so when you are ready to bring a room to life in your own home, you will have the tools to cultivate the luxury and comfort your family has dreamed about.

When someone asks me, "What should I use in this room or that room' my answer is always, "What makes you happy?" Think about the space as your own. What do you enjoy? How will the space be used?

So, what's my style? I can describe it in five words: I use what I like.

In this book, I will refer to two homes where our family has grown and loved and lived. One is in Olive Hill, Kentucky, the town where I was raised. The other is in Redington Shores, Florida. This is our little beach house we use as a family retreat. Each home has its own style, character, and use.

At our beach house near the ocean, I used a palette of blue, grey, pink, and neutral with the idea that these hues would bring the outside in. Some family members painted pieces of art for the walls, while others used their talents to contribute decorative pieces throughout the house. Our first winter at the house, my niece and I were on the beach in our winter jackets, making sand angels in the sand while my nephew helped us gather nature's gifts brought in by the tide.

We couldn't wait to carry those wonderful finds back to the house and use them in our decor. Bringing the outside in makes a home casual and comfy. Margie Goldsmith said it best in Coastal Living Magazine, "I have a sense of place here and from this place, my sense of design becomes part of my soul." I feel the same way at the beach.

On the walls, I used old pictures of my mom at the beach in the 1940s. I love to see the style of the clothing and bathing suits from that period. I also incorporated some of her mid-century modern furniture into the space there. To invite love, comfort, and joy into the space, we placed my mom's quilts (she was a beautiful quilt maker) on display in every room. So, what's my style? I can describe it in five words: I use what I like.

Wrapping yourself in a quilt passed from generation to generation does something for the soul. I love quilts, and I have a collection both from my side of the family and from the family that I married into (as we say in the South). These items can be seen in our home, and they are displayed throughout the photographs in this book.

Try It Out!

Still trying to settle on your unique style? Involve the whole family! Make a style board using a medium-sized cork board (you can find these at any craft store). Place fabric samples (from curtain, sofa, and cushion options), pin photos from books and magazines, paint chips, and wallpaper prints on the board. Include a photo of the area rug, carpet, or your wood flooring as a background. Place the board where all family members will pass it daily. After a couple of weeks, see if everyone agrees with the chosen samples or wants to make adjustments. Children especially love being a part of adult decision-making, because they will live there too!

"Flowers have a unique way of bringing pleasure. They affirm life in so many ways."

—KIMBERLY STEVENS PATTON

COZY FARMHOUSE, FRENCH ELEGANCE, KENTUCKY CHARM

If I really had to pin down my personal style, I think I would describe a harmony between cozy farmhouse, French elegance, and some Kentucky charm. While in Paris France I was in awe of the simplicity of the white-faced buildings with white marble trim that have stood there year after year after year without any change in design.

I have always had a sweet spot for the French style. It is an effortless, minimalist style that grabs your attention. I love the look of dishes displayed on walls.

White dishes and creamy soup tureens are beautiful additions to a space. There's nothing more French than a huge wall display of white plates and platters. Gorgeous!

Buttery yellow is a popular color in the French style, and it pairs beautifully with green or blue. Painted white furniture with aged elegance makes a space look cozy and lived in. In our Olive Hill home, we extended this French feel to the walls with a buttercream paint and white high gloss enamel on the wood trim.

A solid, tan linen fabric looks great as a neutral cover for sofas, ottomans, and chairs. Then, add color with pillows and accessories to brighten the room and reflect your mood. I bought some buttercream and teal flowered chintz draperies for my dining room at an antique store in Florida and was told they were purchased on a shopping trip in France. They are edged in a cream fringe that give the draperies character.

My daughter, Jessi, brought me cream curtains with black flowers and vines that she found when studying in France. I adjusted the length of the curtains to hang six inches above the baseboard, which gives the room a unique twist. This technique also makes for an easy room to clean because the shortened curtains our out of the way when cleaning baseboards or running the vacuum.

You don't have to be a jet setter to emulate the French style at home. With a lot of patience and trips to flea markets, yard sales, and auctions, you can create a quaint French style all your own. Pillows in whites and pastels, toile and ticking, white vases and antique wood -- these are all beautiful French touches that you can incorporate into your own style. But, careful not to overdo the theme. I sometimes see rooms that use fabric on the walls. In a home, you have to be able to breathe, so please take it easy with the fabric. Keep the style light and airy. You can always add to it.

Here's another decorating secret I learned from the French: decorate with what you use daily. Fill a gorgeous, creamy old water pitcher with beautiful flowers. I suggest using wildflowers for a more rustic, farmhouse appeal. The farmhouse style also makes use of white painted furniture with a lived-in look. Don't be afraid of furniture that is a little chipped and worn. It adds character! No farmhouse should be without a farm table, so keep your eyes open for a beautiful wooden table that can fit your loved ones snuggly around it.

> *HOME IS WHERE LOVE RESIDES, MEMORIES ARE CREATED, FRIENDS ALWAYS BELONG, AND LAUGHTER NEVER ENDS.*

The beauty of farmhouse style is that it recognizes no boundaries. It embraces an eclectic mix of periods and aesthetics.

– Kim Leggett

Incorporate a lifestyle shift into your design.

In today's busy world, there are so many demands on our time that it is difficult to find a moment to slow down. Create spaces in your home for enjoying your coffee or tea. I have a favorite cup I use for tea and one I use for coffee. The cup you choose is part of the relaxation process. Incorporate sitting with your cup as a part of your self-care time. Think about how luxurious it feels to sit and drink a cappuccino in a cafe or order a meal in a nice restaurant. Try to invite something new and fresh into your home by creating these spaces for you and your loved ones to sit and enjoy.

BLENDING THE OLD AND THE NEW

My personality is a little bit old and a little bit new. What's your personality like? Your home is a reflection of you, so let your essence come through in your designs. Elevate your home's style by blending pieces from the past with new and contemporary ones. This dissolves a more boring style and pulls the eye to unexpected hints of beauty. New and modern items can keep your home fresh and up to date, while antiques comfort and revitalize the soul. I like to use both old and new pieces in my home to give an eclectic and personalized finish.

> "Mix the humble and the grand, clean moderately with classics, but never forget beauty and comfort."
> —Veere Grenney

Don't be afraid to mix it up. I do recommend purchasing a new and comfortable sofa. This is a great starting point that you can build upon as you are decorating a room. A traditional and high-quality sofa will save you (and your spouse) heartache in the end (take it from someone who has bought six sofas in the last fifteen years). On a limited budget, a sofa is where you want to invest. Buying the right sofa that you will live with for years to come will pay off in the end. Grey and ivory are great neutral colors, and you can always add a pop of color with some beautiful throw pillows. These are easy to find at discounted prices, so you can change them out when you desire.

Mixing old and new, casual and formal, elegant curves and straight lines is an exercise in balance. Follow your instincts. Hone and refine a room until you are satisfied with a look that pleases your soul. Each room's design should produce a good feeling. That's why, even when I see an antique that is beautiful, if I know that it won't support the comfort of my home, I won't choose it.

Mixing old and new china makes a lasting memory of a unique dining experience.

BUILDING YOUR NEST

Nesting, it seems is a human instinct. When I was 27 years old, I became pregnant with our first daughter, Jessi. This was when nesting really kicked in for me. As I cleaned our home top to bottom, going over our furniture piece by piece, I felt like a bird preparing her nest for chicks.

For me, here's how preparing the nest for children went:

- Clean the home.

- Rid the house of anything potentially harmful.

- Set up the nursery.

- Wash and dry all clothing items and blankets in a mild detergent.

- After the baby comes, trips will be harder to take, so stock up the pantry, freezer, and refrigerator.

- Keep necessities close at hand. Knowing where things are after the baby comes will be a welcome reprieve.

Every Room is for Everyone

As you are designing your home, keep in mind who your home is for. Don't design a picture-perfect room that no one is allowed to walk through. After all, these are the living spaces where we make our lives. We want our children to feel welcome and for the family to enjoy one another's company. When our girls were young, we used every inch of our house for play.

When thrift shopping for a new room, pick up old end and coffee tables that have a few scratches. This gives them character, and you won't have to worry about the kids ruining them.

Who remembers being dragged to BLAIR parties by your mother? Growing up in the 60s, this was a common occurrence for me. My mother would insist that I come along, and inevitably all the neighborhood kids would be there, too. While the mothers talked home decor, we kids would entertain ourselves ransacking the homes of the hostesses or playing games until the party was mercifully over.

Don't hide fragile items away in china cabinets. Bring your finery out and put it to good use! Teach your babies not to touch fragile objects. They are going to have to learn sometime! When my kids were young, I never removed anything from our tables. To this day, we still have those special pieces that were on tables and nightstands from when the girls first started walking.

When someone asks me, "What should I use in this room or that room" my answer is always, "What makes you happy?" Think about the space as your own. What do you enjoy? How will the space be used?

Organization and Just Saying 'No'

If your life is like mine, you don't have time to spend searching for that important paper or bill that needs to be paid. Nothing frustrates me more than not being able to find the pair of jeans I planned to wear or a jacket as I'm running out the door. Being organized allows for space and relaxation. Over the years, I've gathered some tools that help keep the home organized:

1. When you purchase new items for the home (whether a lawn mower, TV, or kitchen appliance), save the receipts in one file. Keep warranty information in the file as well. If something goes wrong with your purchases, you will know exactly where to find the return or warranty information.

2. As you walk in the door with your mail in hand, don't set the mail down any old place. Either sort through the mail immediately, or have a designated basket on your desk where mail to-be-sorted can go. I will discuss RSVPs later in the party section because one should respond immediately, and then place all event invitations into a file according to date.

3. Each season (we have all four here in Kentucky!), pull out all of your clothing and go through it, piece by piece. If something hasn't been worn in a while or doesn't make you feel great, place it in a donation bag. With children, this is especially important because there will likely be plenty that they have outgrown by the end of each season.

Less Is More

Some say, "less is more." It absolutely can be, especially in a retreat space like an oceanfront home. Use pieces that you need and nothing more. A clutter-free area gives you room to breathe! With the ocean on the horizon, what more does one need to look at and entertain your thoughts? The same can be true of your home, even without the ocean view. Life flows more easily within a home if you keep things organized and free of unused stuff.

It can be very difficult, especially for a parent, to go through and throw away things that once brought enjoyment into the home. However, a good clear out is called for every now and then. I love to clean my home room by room. After each room is finished, I shut the door behind me, giving me a sense of accomplishment before I move to the next. Each season, once the house is completely clean, I go through Willie's and my wardrobes and discard everything we don't love anymore or didn't wear last year.

If you don't love it, you won't miss it, and you can let someone else enjoy it. Churches are a great place to give away clothing. I take my donations to a local women's shelter. Every few months, I enjoy walking through my home and gathering items that are outdated, no longer excite me, or don't serve a purpose, and I donate them appropriately.

Remember to Say 'No!'

I cannot emphasize this enough: say no to babysitting others' junk. Children leaving the nest are often slow to retrieve things stored at the family home because they don't yet have a space of their own. However, the longer you keep things, the less likely your children are to need them. Things go out of style or are replaced with updated versions. Photos and artwork take up a lot of space. This can be a delicate situation but remember that your space is your own. Don't let it become overtaken by others' unwanted stuff.

Great Design Sparks Creativity

I do not believe that great design is only for the rich and famous. Great design is something that tells a story, that writes the message of your home. A house that is designed well encourages you to be creative. If a corner can be made cozy or high ceilings invite a unique chandelier, respond to these calls to create! Let the wheels turn in your mind and start drafting the vision for your own, unique space.

Design is a challenge and a journey. It can't be rushed. But, when a space comes together to create the feeling of home, the days of planning, scouring flea markets, and DIY-ing will be worth it. When you find that special farm table, the perfect lamps, those modern club chairs, the composition of the space begins to come together around these pieces, your personality shining through, the feeling is magical.

Once you get into it, you will find yourself thinking nonstop about ways to make your home your own. You'll daydream about that perfect piece of furniture to complete a room. You'll be waking up early on a Saturday morning to hit the flea market to find it. Even without a specific piece in mind, a new find or an interesting accessory inspires me to rearrange an entire room. It's all about what sparks your creativity. When making your home your own, surround yourself with beautiful things. Build a timeless and versatile framework that allows you to play with color, texture, and pattern over time.

FLEA MARKETS: A DESIGNER'S FAVORITE PASTIME

During my teen years, I was drawn to older pieces of furniture in other's homes or in thrift stores. My dad shared my love of old junk, and he would often trade a piece of our furniture for an older version of it at the Jockey Ground Flea Market. Many Thursday mornings, I would stand next to my dad, with my arm around his neck, riding in his old '58 Chevy truck toward Jockey Ground for a day of buying, trading, and selling. We would stay for hours.

Les Puces de Saint-Ouen, Paris, France

To this day, I still love flea markets and tag sales. Buying and trading is in my blood, and I always find beauty in someone else's junk. For me, it's a stress antidote as well. I find there's no satisfaction like a good junk store fix when I'm having a bad day or need to get out of the house for a few. The key to finding treasures is challenging the imagination with beautiful finds. Don't let yourself be distracted by a couple of stains or an undesirable finish. Look past the surface flaws to see the shape, the detailing, and what drew you to the piece in the first place. Take it home and make it your own. A bench can be upholstered in a new and updated fabric. A peeling finish on wood can be sanded down and repainted.

It's not always necessary to buy more stuff. Just thinking creatively about your home can trigger new ideas and satisfy the soul. John Barrymore says, "Happiness sneaks in through a door you didn't know you left open."

Knowing the story behind the finds you bring into your home is half the fun. Ask the antique store owner what he or she may know about the piece and the history behind it. Do your research, too! Learning an item's history: how and when it was used, and for what purpose, makes for good conversation.

> IT'S NOT ALWAYS NECESSARY TO BUY MORE STUFF. JUST THINKING CREATIVELY ABOUT YOUR HOME CAN TRIGGER NEW IDEAS AND SATISFY THE SOUL.

Incorporating Heirlooms into Your Design

My sweet Aunt Hazel bought an old china cabinet from a neighbor. It was mahogany in color, with two glass doors on top, one drawer in the middle, and two wooden doors below. I think this was the first time I realized that receiving something that someone else had used and loved actually made the piece more special. One day, when I was visiting her home, she whispered in a low voice, "When I am finished with this cabinet, I will leave it for you." Many years later, I inherited it. I still feel her love when I walk by it or open a drawer to retrieve a beautiful quilt.

My Aunt Ina Kiser (we pronounced it, "Eye-Nee") loved pretty things, and her home was a showcase of her taste. From her, I became the caretaker of a beautiful set of china, a washboard, quilts, a slicer, and other dishes. She entrusted me to keep these items, preserve them, and hold the knowledge of our family history and what each piece represents. It's not the pieces themselves, but it is the hands that held them, worked with them, washed and loved them. As the keeper of this knowledge, I have surrounded myself, my husband, and my children with these things that are close to my heart.

Vignettes, Step-by-Step

As much as I enjoy designing a home, an outdoor space, or a room, I love designing little vignettes throughout a house. These little design snapshots are an opportunity to tell a story, spark conversation, and evoke a feeling, often without the viewer even realizing the message you have shared. If you have never heard of vignettes, you have probably seen them. You may even have created them in your own home without realizing it.

When I build a vignette, I start with three elements and a flat surface. I choose a table and a few pretty items that I love to look at. Start piling on objects until you like the look. Each item creates interest in how it interacts with the objects around it. Wood and glass work well together. I also love the sparkle of a silver tray with a picture frame, a piece of mouth-blown glass, or an heirloom piece from a special family member. The shimmer of glass or a reflection in a mirrored surface makes me smile. A wooden table adds warmth. Candlesticks lend height. If the vignette ever starts looking too busy, take off your least favorite piece. Often, we've only gone too far by one touch.

Think of your vignette as a pocket-sized table arrangement that tells a story about you and your home. The best thing about a vignette is that it invites conversation. Make sure to include something unusual or interesting in your vignette. A medal your grandfather received in the service, alongside a photo of him in uniform, will engage all ages. The styling and aesthetic will draw the eye, and the personal items will spark conversation. Instantly, your home becomes interactive for your guests and loved ones.

Have a small table in need of some TLC? Try some trendy printed fabric as a floor-length table skirt. You don't even need to hem it! Use this colorful, printed tablecloth as the surface for your vignette. Start with small framed photos, a stack of books, and a lamp. Add an acrylic or silver tray under these objects, and voila! you've created a stunning vignette.

Three Rules When Creating a Vignette:

1. Display items in odd numbers. Even numbers can look too matchy.

2. Use objects of varying heights, including candles and glass cylinders.

3. Use different textures and colors to tell a story.

My dad, Clifford Stevens (known by friends as Richie) was a self-employed plumber, machinist, and electrician. He learned his trades while serving an eight-year stint in the United States Navy. Dad was stationed in Pearl Harbor on the ship The Utah the morning of December 7, 1941, when the naval base was attacked by the Imperial Japanese Navy Air Service. This attack, later known as the Battle of Pearl Harbor, led the United States into World War II. For my family, the attack caused a different kind of turmoil.

My mother and my sister, who was two weeks old at the time, were living in Long Beach, California, near the naval base, when news spread of the attack. Blackouts were common, and it wasn't clear whether there would be additional attacks on the west coast of the U.S., so the Navy sent my mother and sister home to Kentucky to await the news if Dad was alive or killed in action. For six weeks, my mother suffered the nightmare of not knowing. My dad survived but did not return home. Instead, he remained in the Navy another four years to fight in the war. The women of the greatest generation were strong women that had to raise their children alone and keep peace at the home place while their husbands were away at war.

CHAPTER SIX
DESIGN TIPS: ROOM BY ROOM

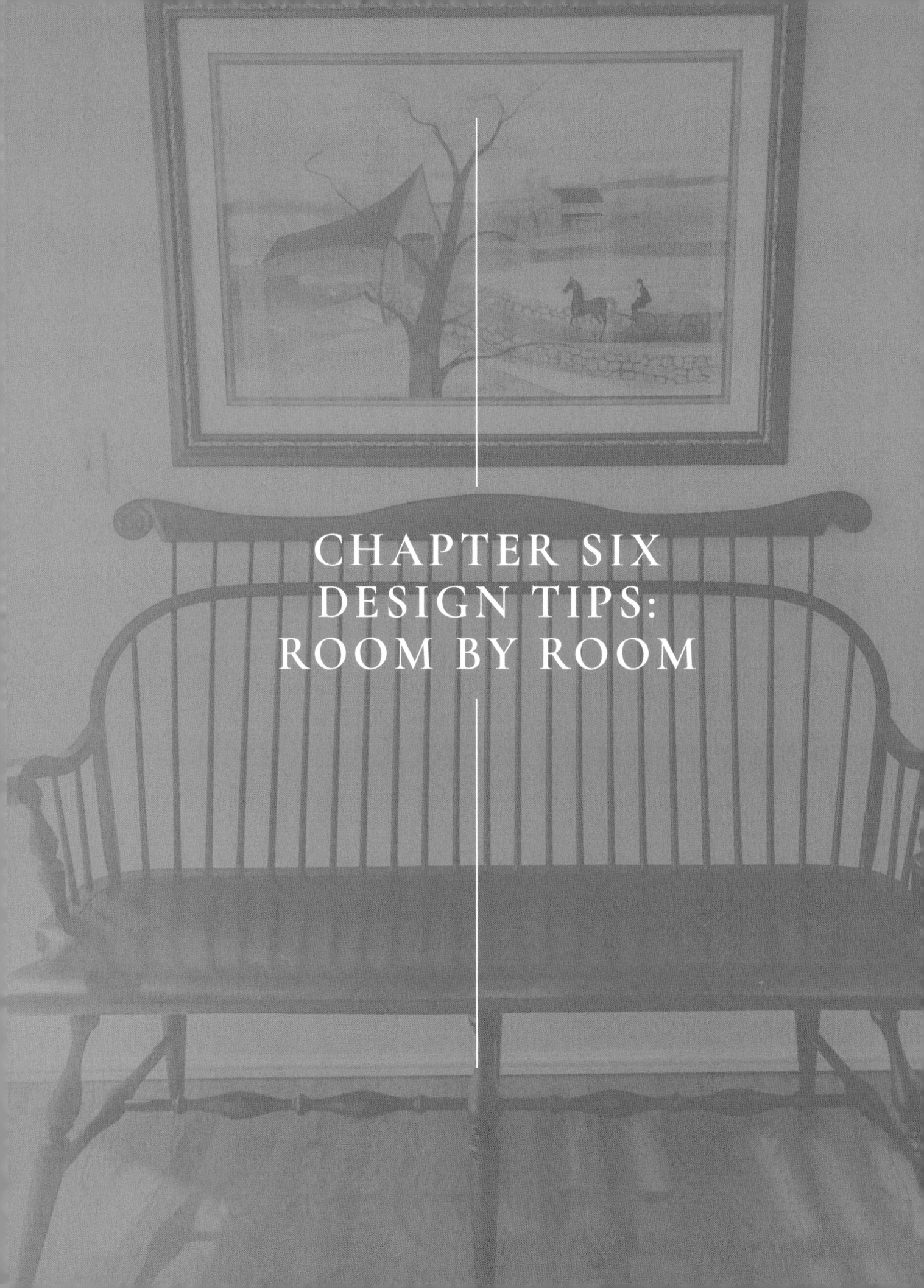

Starting From Scratch

If you are working with a fixer-upper, starting from scratch can seem daunting. It's also a great gift because you can design your home exactly the way you want it from the beginning. Here are a few tips when starting with a fixer-upper:

1. Work on the walls and floor first. Once they are clean and beautiful, you can start filling the space with things that create the home feeling you want.

2. Unless the baseboards are wide and beautiful, replace them. This is one way to give new life to an old room.

3. Starting with a lovely color or a beautiful, soft white, you then build upon this palette to craft the perfect space that you and yours will love for years to come.

4. Remember that the personality is in the details. Build a beautiful, clean canvas and then decorate the room with beautiful things that make you smile.

The Kitchen is the Heart of the Home

Very often, the kitchen is the heart of the home. It is a room where everyone gathers. It is the conference room where children share about their day: good or not so good. To accommodate so much living, a kitchen takes careful planning and diligent honing.

Be brave! You can step out of the neutral when designing your kitchen. Choose a different trim color than white. If you decide on neutral walls and trim, use spots of color throughout the room. Adding color on a neutral palate allows you to take risks and change with the seasons.

When choosing cabinets, take your time. Weigh your options because your selection will be in place for a long time. For appliances, stainless steel is a safe finish because it is neutral and will go with almost any cabinet finish you choose. For countertops, I love, love, love Carrara marble with gold or silver faucets placed on a wide, white farmhouse sink. If you have visited many hundred-year-old historic homes, you can still find the marble looking its best.

The Not-too-Formal Dining Room

Often, the dining room is the most unused room in a house. Allow your dining space to reflect your personality and the kinds of celebrations that you will host in the space.

If you have a more casual style, almost anything goes! Set up a pretty wooden table, buy the right number of chairs for your family (they don't have to match!), and ta dah, you have a dining room. Start keeping an eye out for a cabinet to store your dishes. I love the look of open shelving, especially in a smaller space. White dishes can be dressy or casual, and they never distract from the food or accessories you use to set your table. If you are lucky enough to have a square dining room, try a large round table that seats six or more, and you will be surprised at how well a group fits in the space.

Use family photos sparingly throughout the house to incorporate the love of family into your design. There is something truly special about having photos of friends and family members who have passed near you. Our dining room has framed photos wall to wall of the people who have had an influence on our lives. I think of our photo wall as a tree, with different branches growing in different directions. We all come from the same roots, learning from our elders, before taking one of the many paths available to us.

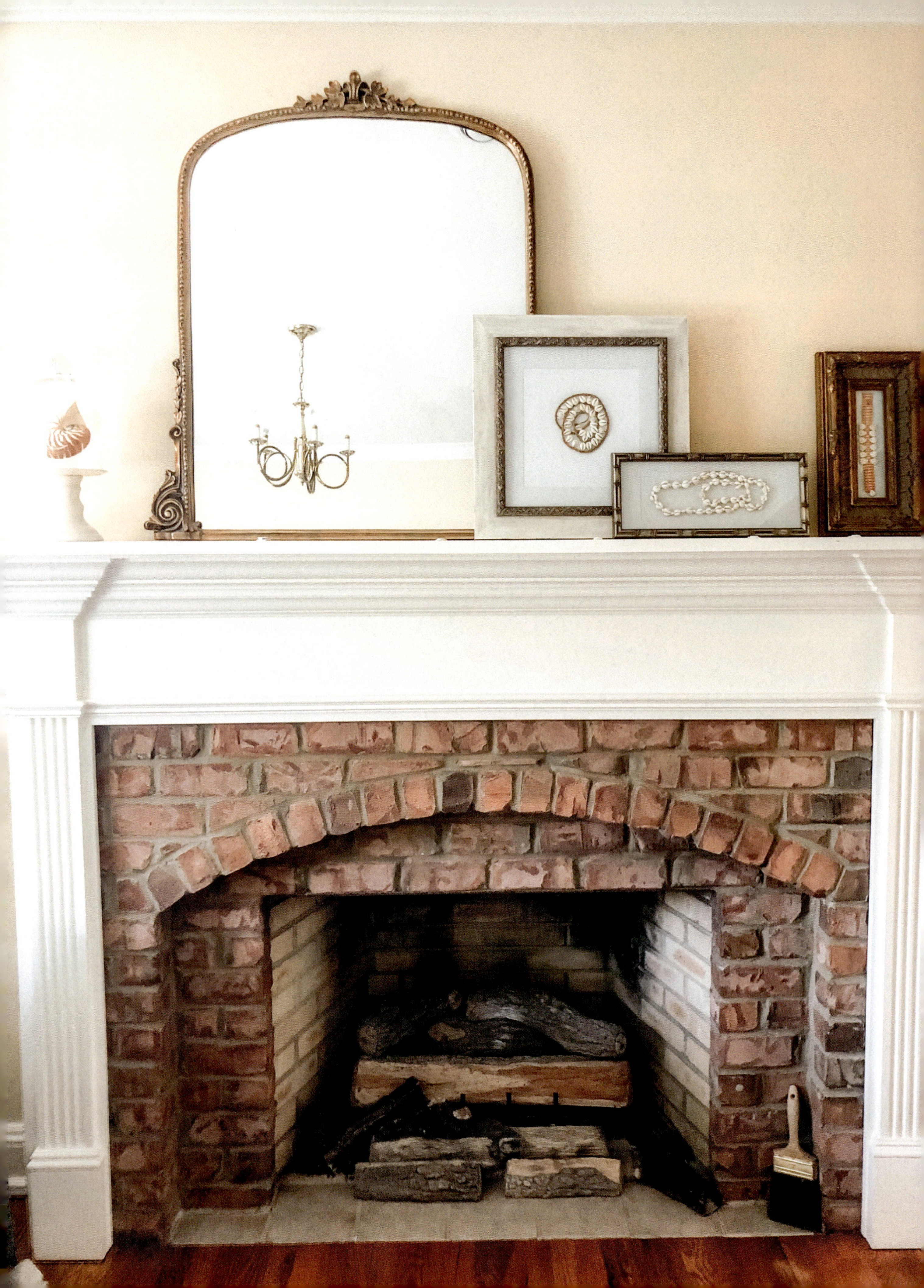

Books Make Great Accessories.

In our home, I designed several walls of built-in shelving to provide more storage. A bookshelf is a dominant element in a room, and it is a great way to display beautiful objects. Try painting the walls behind the shelves a different color to showcase the books and other objects displayed. Some people don't love the look of book covers all mixed together. With one client, we solved this problem by covering their books with white paper and painting the wall behind the books in the same shade. Personally, I love the look of various book covers stacked and standing tall.

Set Your Walls Free!

Who wants shy walls? Let flowers grow with pretty wallpaper. I know what you are thinking: we baby boomers watched our mothers sweat over glue and wallpaper only to rip it off a few years later. But great news! Wall art today comes pre-pasted, and some are easily removable. Powder rooms are a great place to experiment with florals. It's simple enough that you can create a totally new look with a weekend job that will make you smile every time you visit the space.

Growing up in the South with strong women around me shaped me deeply. My mother was the epitome of a strong Southern woman. Life wasn't easy for her, but she never complained and always made the best of the hand she was dealt.

She hung wallpaper, embroidered towels and pillowcases, and set out beautiful flowerpots on our front porch. These small, colorful adjustments seemed to us kids to be total redecorations, and that idea stuck with me. I love making small additions or changes to excite my family.

For as long as I can remember, my mom had a standing appointment at the beauty shop in town on Fridays. I always went with her, and she would give me a few dollars to go next door to the dime store and buy candy or a new outfit for my Barbie doll. Mom, like all the women in our family, always looked her best. The women of her generation were classy, they wore hats to church with their very best suit or dress. I can honestly say that I never witnessed my mother wearing a tee shirt. Wow! haven't times changed! My mom took me to the First Baptist Church where I was a member of the JR choir. Fifty years later I still have my choir pin and will never forget one of my Sunday school-teachers [Miss Blevins] who taught me how important it was to learn the Bible verse John 3:16 KJV.

Hospitality was especially important to the women in my family. I loved that whenever we would stop by to visit an aunt, we would be greeted with a warm welcome and a piece of dessert with a cup of coffee or a glass of sweet tea. Sweet tea reminds me of my family and of the Sunday dinner that my mother-in-law Alma cooked each week. Alma's Sunday dinner wasn't any three-course meal. She would throw down a spread as if the President was coming by.

Incorporate Happy

I love painting a ceiling blue with a high gloss finish. This looks especially great on a porch or in a room with a lot of light. The sun's reflection on the blue gloss ceiling takes on the look of sunbeams dancing on water. This is a great way to incorporate the feeling of happy, sun-filled days on a beach vacation. You can even add a seagrass rug for summer fun and a warm soft one for colder days.

Mixing Textures (and a Love Affair with the Color White)

I love mixing metal with white pieces. I bought a metal storage bin that I placed next to my white sofa for a little mix up. Use ferns as a softening touch near metal. Layer after layer, you are adding the detail and texture that makes a room a delightful place to be. White marble in the kitchen adds elegance. Add charm with pretty, antique tablecloths and linens to soften the space. White dishes in a painted cabinet look clean and fresh.

Mixing Patterns

Are you afraid of patterns? Especially more than one? There is an old rule that patterns make a space look "busy." But there is a secret to mixing patterns successfully: stay in the same color family! It's fun to mix patterns and textiles by using two or three patterns together. Cover the back of a chair with one fabric, and then use a burlap coffee sack fabric with stamped print on the seat of the chair. I don't recommend using more than three patterns in one space, but otherwise, feel free to experiment! A great way to play with pattern is to choose a neutral sofa and then add pillows in a cheerful pattern (or two!). Cushions and other accessories can easily be changed if you want to adapt the look.

Another way to introduce pattern is with a wallpaper. This can completely change the look of a room. If you aren't a fan of wall coverings, that's ok. There are lots of ways to incorporate color into a room.

"There are hundreds of variations of the color white - some slightly blue, others with a touch of pink or green or yellow. But no matter the hint or hue, the essence of all shades of white is something clean, pure, and fresh."

*- The Cottage Journal,
Cottages of White*

Window Treatments

For seven years after we built our home, we did not have any window treatments or coverings on our windows. I just didn't know what I wanted, and it is such a big commitment when you start sinking hundreds of dollars into a window covering, you're not absolutely sure about. When I was growing up, my mom used beige silk pleated draperies all through the house, and she kept them for twenty years after I left home to marry. She couldn't afford to redo the window treatments every ten years, so she played it safe with a neutral color. In my own home, I have found that the window treatments I like best are plantation shutters or wide, slatted blinds finished in soft white. They now make them in four-inch slats, which is a dream come true. The wider slats offer a wider view of the outside, they are very easy to clean, and they allow total control of how much light comes through the windows. Wider slat blinds are also more contemporary in style and can modernize an older home.

Making a Room Look Larger

I'd like to share a little something about small rooms. If you can't see the edges of the room, then it will appear smaller than it is. So, when measuring for an area rug, leave about 12" or more on the sides for hardwood to peak out. If the floor is tile, try using a larger size tile to make the room feel larger. A standard 12" tile can make a room look cramped, whereas a 16 or 18" tile can give the space a much larger feeling. This is because of the grout lines between tiles. The fewer visible grout lines, the less busy the space will be, and the larger the room will feel.

Kim's Tip: When I was ready to purchase sofas for the beach house, my niece Christy had a brilliant idea. We first laid out the dimensions of the sofa and other furniture in the space using masking tape on the floor. This allowed us to change around our furniture without any of the heavy lifting! It also gave us the opportunity to decide how large a sofa would be appropriate within the space.

Trim Work

Trim work is a language that communicates style even without being a feature of a room. You can add trim work to make your home more formal or use it less to suit a more laid-back taste. If you are struggling with a room, crisp molding can often create a complete look.

Think about the colors that attract you in magazines and other homes you've visited. My sister, Toni, chose to stain all of her wood trim in her home a dark mahogany and then paired the trim with a light oak stain on the floors. For her home, both choices were right on the mark. In our home, Willie and I decided to go with a white oil-based paint on our woodwork, just like my parents had in our home growing up. In early spring, I remember my mom sprucing up the moldings and doors with a new can of white paint to cover the fingerprints and other unwanted marks.

If you are at a loss for what to do with your trim work, try painting your woodwork and moldings white and staining floors a medium to dark mahogany or chestnut stain. In our home, we also painted the kick plates on the stairs white to match the doors and trim surrounding them. We then stained the steps and handrail to match the stain on the floors. As a finishing touch, we painted the balusters white to match the trim, achieving a balance of heavy and light in the space.

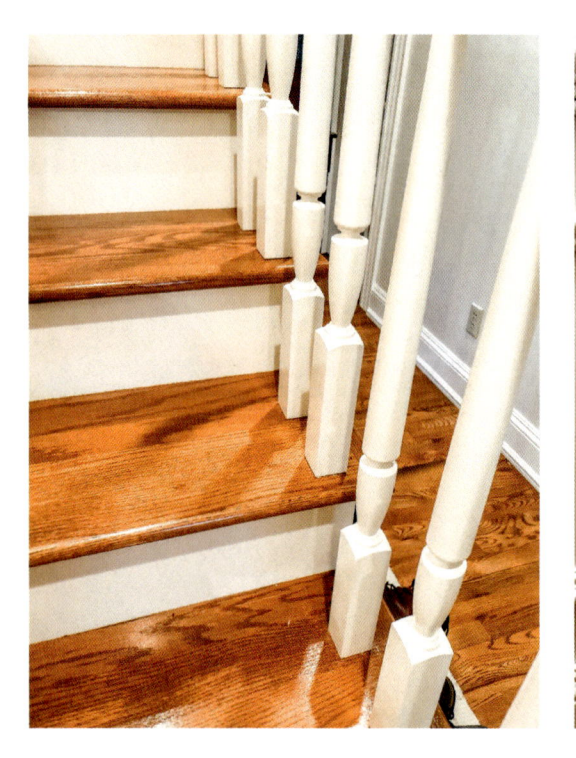

CULTIVATING YOUR OUTDOOR SPACE

One of the most important places for socializing in a Kentucky home is on the porch. On a hot summer day, rather than sitting indoors in the air conditioning, I grew up sitting on porches and decks visiting with friends and neighbors. Not so long ago, sipping iced tea and sharing stories on the porch was the way to be. The porch was a means of conversation. We looked forward to cool summer nights, grilling outdoors, and enjoying others' company.

Creating an outdoor space, whether it's a covered porch, deck, or patio is a great way to entice loved ones to gather, share stories, and make new memories. Outdoor spaces can easily be changed with the seasons by buying new pillows to spruce up the gliders and deck chairs.

Many weekends during summer months, you will find my husband and me scouring flea markets and bringing new finds into our backyard. An old barn tool or an antique dolly looks beautiful in a flower bed. We purchased a very old iron baby bed with a little rust and some white paint remaining on it. We covered it with clear coat protectant to seal the beautiful patina. It turned out so beautiful that I used it at our youngest daughter's baby shower to display the gifts. I have to admit, people loved it! After the shower, we brought the bed into the garden and filled it with dirt. In the spring, we plan to sew Black Eyed Susans in the "bed" for unique garden interest.

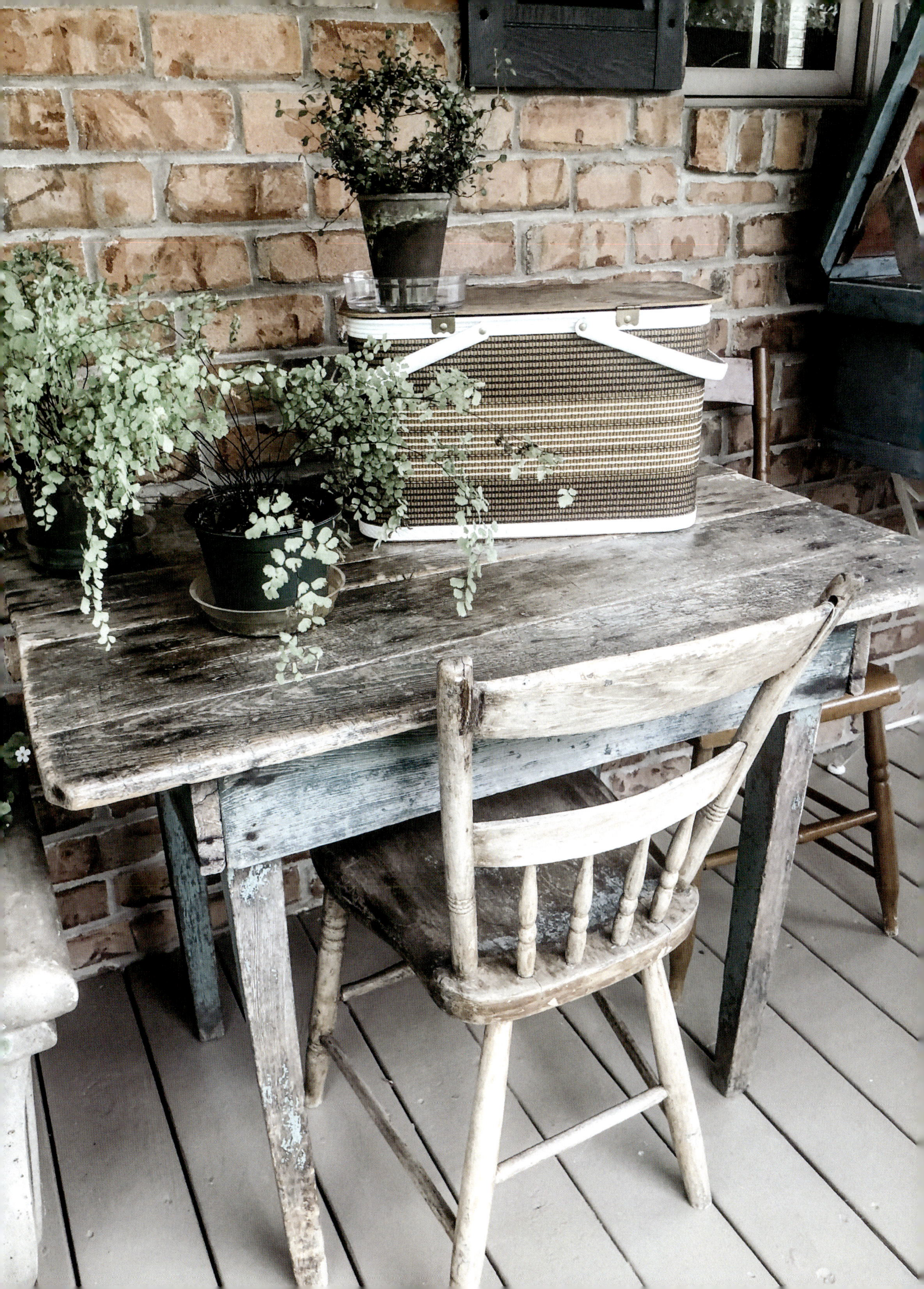

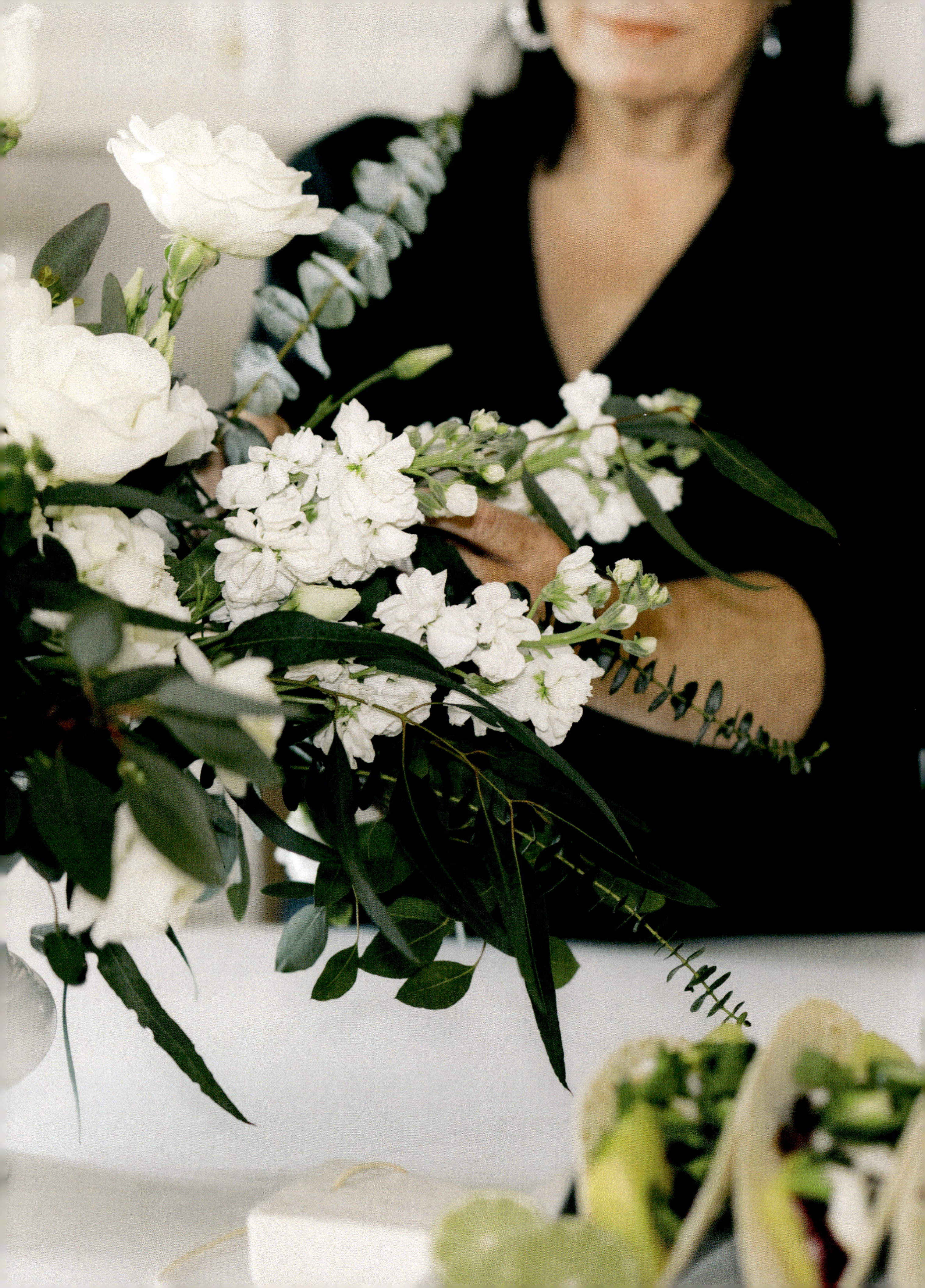

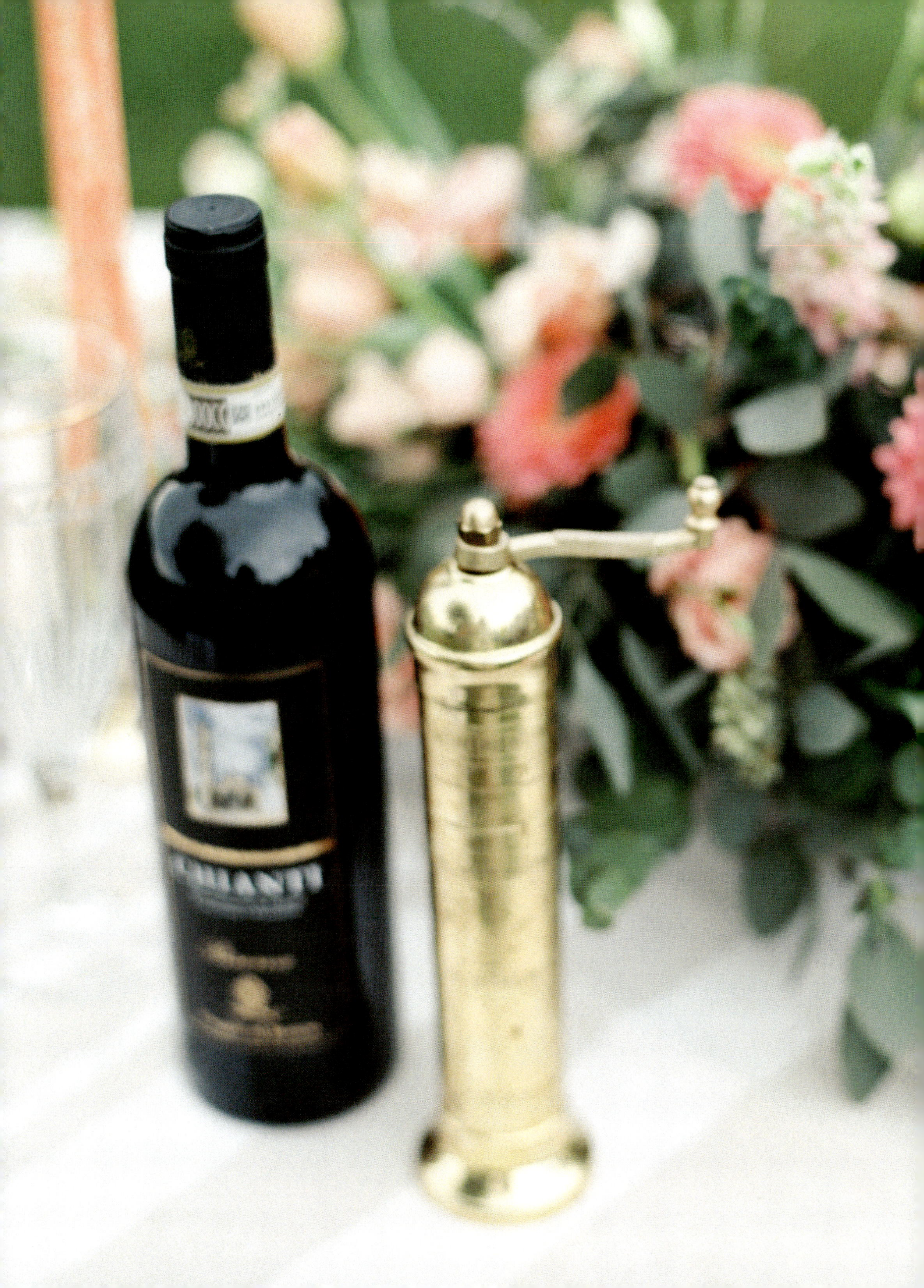
CHIANTI

My friend Mary has a bottle tree in her back yard. It is a perfect example of an interesting piece you can make at home. To make this work of art, you use rebar as a base and add rebar branches. If you aren't an accomplished welder, enlist a little help putting the base together. Then, start collecting bottles from your favorite occasions (weddings, celebrating a new job, or an anniversary) or colorful bottles you see in antique shops. Different styles and colors look lovely together and add height and interest in your garden, especially in the winter months.

ORIGINALITY IS KEY WHEN PUTTING YOUR IDEAS TO WORK. BY USING DIFFERENT AND UNUSUAL FINDS, YOU CREATE CHARACTER AND INDIVIDUALITY. ALLOW YOUR TRUE COLORS TO SHINE THROUGH. THIS IS A PROCESS YOU CAN'T MESS UP.

The Ways Flowers Affect Our Lives

Cultivating flowers is a nurturing and beautiful thing to do for the very young to the young at heart. Choosing flowers from your garden and contemplating how to incorporate them indoors is a relaxing and rewarding process. In the garden, I usually choose white, purple, and yellow flowers.

Flowers affirm life for me in so many ways. To my taste, a loose bouquet of wildflowers is delightful. I also like to bunch a lot of one type of flower into a tight, elegant nosegay. Anything that holds water can be a vase. I use everything from rusty cans to colored glass containers. Even a lipstick lid can be a tiny vase for a single stem. Keep flower water fresh by using a few drops of chlorine bleach.

When tulips appear at the florist, I choose white ones to bring home and place around the house. They are the first rays of warmth in the spring, signaling winter to leave us for another year.

Flowers have a unique way of bringing pleasure and luxury into the home. I have often said, "When I win the lottery, I will have fresh flowers through my home every day." Really, bringing home fresh flowers doesn't have to be expensive, and they can bring so much enjoyment to our daily lives. If you are expecting a guest to stay for the evening, it is a sweet sentiment to place a small vase of flowers on their nightstand or in the bathroom. They will greatly appreciate it.

I have always tried to instill in my daughters how important it is to be the person who shows up when someone is in need. I learned this lesson watching my parents and their families do whatever needed to be done to help someone who is hurting.

When a neighbor would pass away, my mother and a friend would walk from house to house collecting money to buy an arrangement of flowers to send to the funeral home. Our neighbors weren't rich, but they would always open their pockets when a friend was in need. When I was older, it was my turn to walk around the hill and collect the flower money. Red Griffey handed me the largest amount we had ever received from one person. As he handed me the five-dollar bill, he said "maybe when I die, someone will send me flowers". Again, flowers serve us in various ways. They can cheer us up when we are sad, and they have a long-term positive effect on moods.

Specifically, study participants reported feeling less depressed, anxious and agitated after receiving flowers, and demonstrated a higher sense of enjoyment and life satisfaction. The presence of flowers led to increased contact with family and friends.

Brighten a Winter Day with a Little Sunshine

If you are like me, your soul needs a little sunshine. I love the colors and crisp evenings of autumn but, when snow begins to blanket our landscape, I find myself craving fresh flowers to brighten our home. Bringing beautiful blossoms into our space, especially when the weather is grey outside, lifts our spirits and brings ease to the soul. As a gardener and a designer, I notice that new growth in whatever form I can get it, instantly shifts my mood.

YOUR HOME THROUGH THE SEASONS

HOLIDAYS AND PARTIES

Holidays are and have always been an exciting time in our family. I want to share with you some fun and uplifting things to do for each of our holidays. Starting with one of my favorites.

Valentine's Day

St. Valentine's Day is the day we celebrate love and friendship. We send messages of love and affection to our sweetheart, family, and friends. Couples honor one another with cards, flowers, and gifts, and spend time together recognizing their love for each other. We teach our children to love and respect everyone, and it is such fun to get to express that love on Valentine's Day.

Here is a fun and easy craft that you can make with loved ones of any age: Valentine's Day Cards. Gather together card stock, ribbon, and any decorations you like. Spread the items on the kitchen table to surprise the kids when they get home from school. This is a photo of Valentine cards that Jessi and Holli made when they were of grade school age.

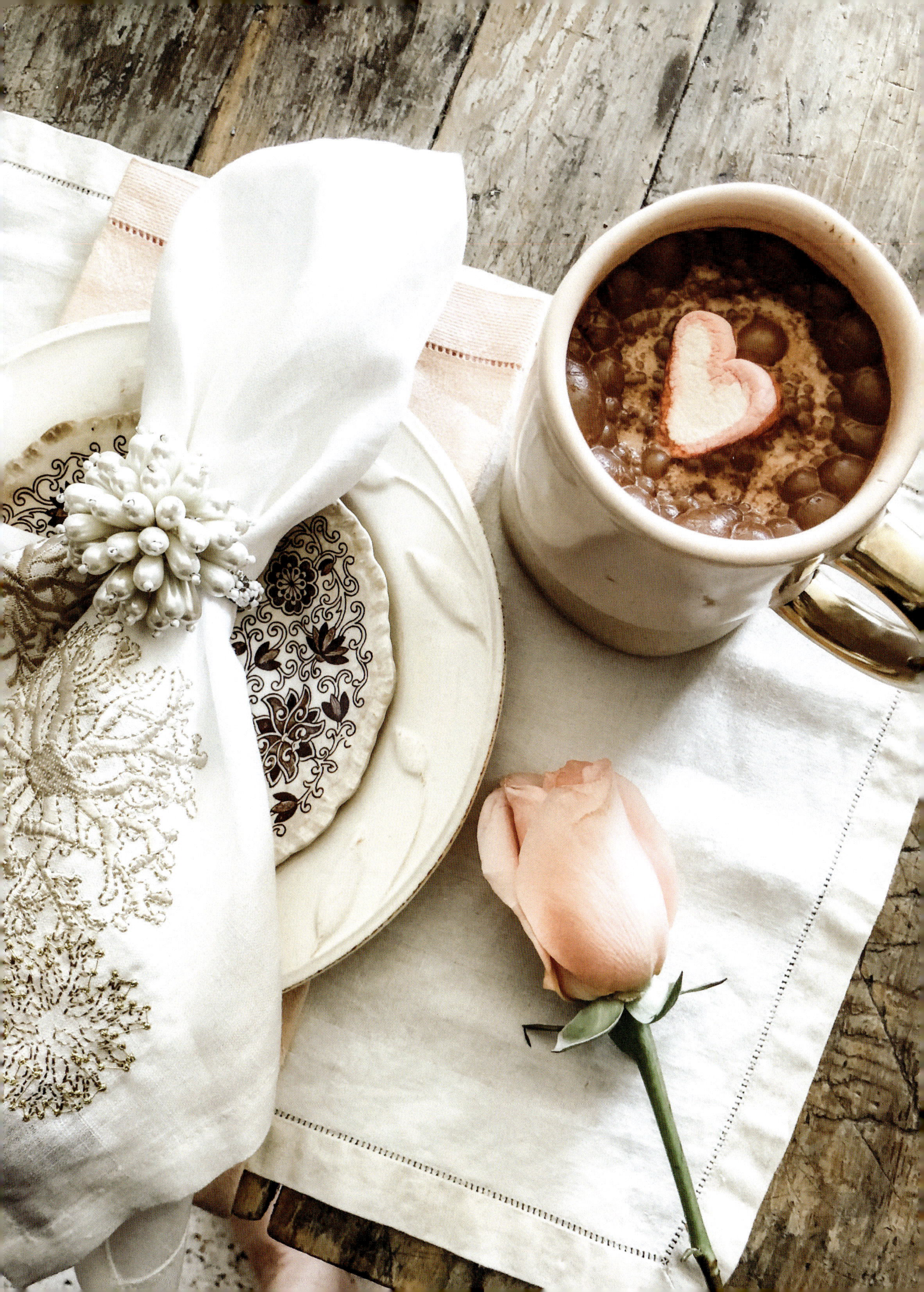

Easter

The centerpiece for mom's Easter table was always stalks of celery standing tall in a beautiful glass. My mother always baked a ham and turkey breast, with mashed potatoes, cole slaw, and green beans for this wonderful holiday.

59

Tissue Easter Eggs

1. Choose a napkin with a small print.

2. Tear the napkin into one-inch pieces. Ragged edges are ok!

3. With a pin or small nail, puncture a hole in each end of the egg. Hold the egg over the sink, and blow the yolk out. Allow the egg to dry overnight to make sure the inside is as clean and dry as possible.

4. Place small pieces of torn napkins on the egg, one at a time. Use rubber cement to apply the pieces.

5. When the egg is completely covered with paper, use a clean craft brush to smooth all wrinkles and flatten edges.

6. Place egg on a wire rack or in an empty egg carton to dry for about 24 hours.

You now have beautiful eggs to enjoy and share with friends and family.

Kentucky Derby

The Kentucky Derby is always held on the first Saturday in May. This is the first leg of horse racings triple crown, and has been described as the most exciting two minutes in sports. Kentucky has always enjoyed a love affair with horses. Be it beautiful bluegrass farms, the charm of Keeneland, and Churchill Downs, or the excitement of the fasig-tipton horse auctions, the attraction is alive and well in the Commonwealth. Wearing hats at the Derby is every woman's chance to express her inner Southern belle, according to the annual horse race's website, which provides guidelines and gentle suggestions for women's attire. The crowning glory of a Southern Belle's ensemble? A standout hat.

Derby Pie

1/2 cup butter
1 cup granulated sugar
1/2 cup flour
2 eggs
1 teaspoon real vanilla extract
1/2 cup chocolate chips
1 Pillsbury pie crust

Mix 1/2 cup butter melted with 2 eggs and vanilla. Add sugar and mix well. Stir in chocolate chips. Pour mixture into piecrust and bake in 350-degree oven for 35-40 minutes till golden brown.

Mint Julip

3 fresh mint leaves
1 tablespoon Mint Simple Syrup
Crushed ice
1 1/2 to 2 tablespoons (1 ounce) bourbon
1 (4-inch) cocktail straw or coffee stirrer
1 fresh mint sprig
powdered sugar (optional)

Place mint leaves and Mint Simple Syrup in a chilled julep cup. Gently press leaves against cup with back of spoon to release flavors. Pack cup tightly with crushed ice; pour bourbon over ice. Insert straw, place mint sprig directly next to straw, and serve immediately. Sprinkle with powdered sugar, if desired.

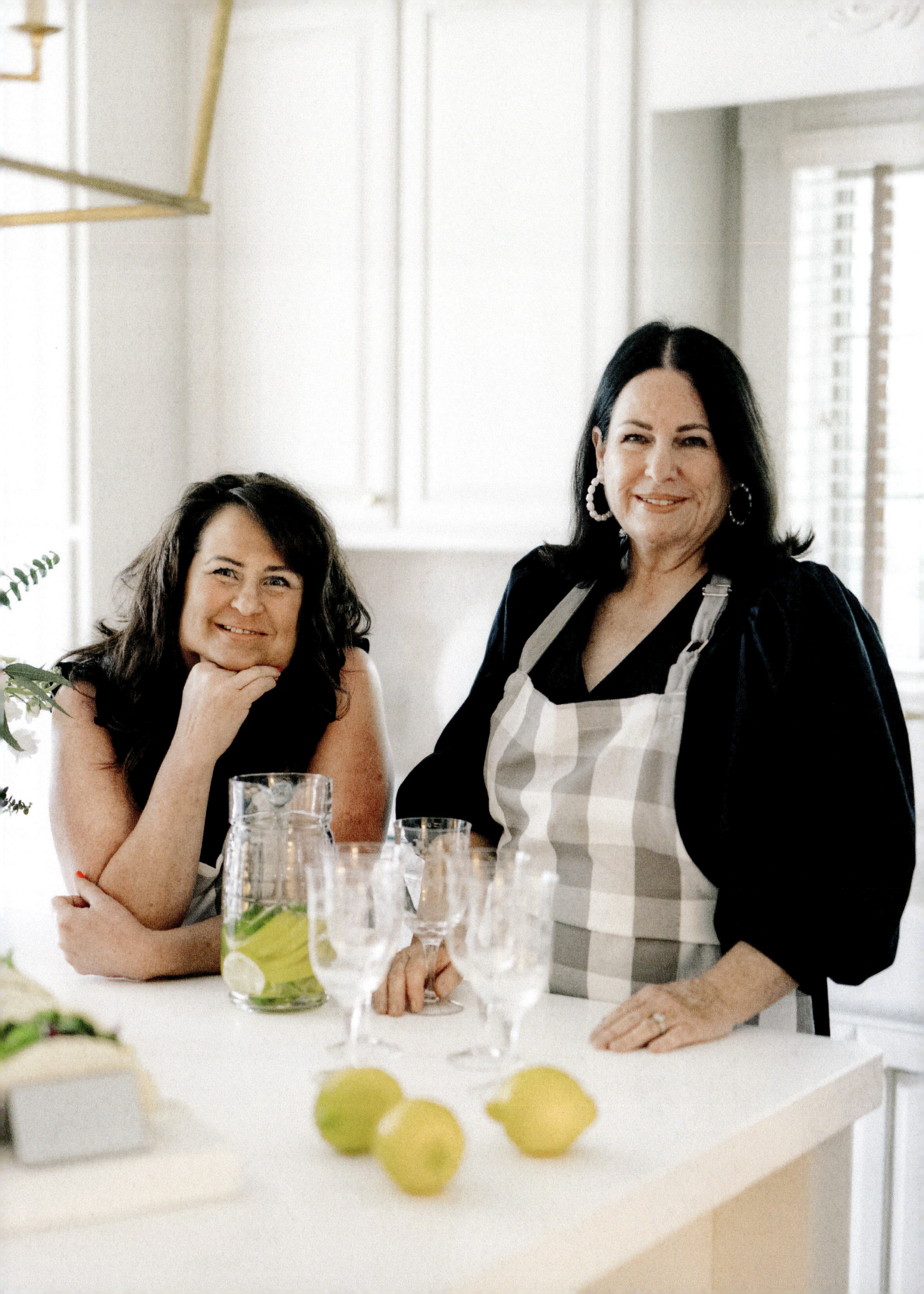

Fish Taco Recipe

Ingredients:
Miso Glazed Cod (Costco)
Pineapple
Shredded lettuce
Shredded purple cabbage
Cilantro
Jalapeno peppers
Red salsa
Green salsa
Soft Taco Shells

1. Bake Miso Glazed Cod for 30 minutes in a 400-degree oven. Remove and let stand two minutes to rest while warming taco shells.

2. Assemble tacos with pineapple slices, purple cabbage, lettuce, jalapeno peppers, salsa, and cheese.

Enjoy!

Summer Memories

In the 1960s, life seemed sweet and simple to me, especially in the summertime. A bicycle with high handlebars, streamers, and a banana seat was of utmost importance to us girls. We played with Barbies and had jacks tournaments that lasted for hours. We spent our days loafing at the bowling alley and the slot car track that my Uncle Toofer owned. He had a large display case filled with slot cars that children could purchase and run on the tracks. One day, my mom and I stopped in to visit Uncle Toofer at the racetrack, and he let me pick out which car I wanted. I chose a Bat mobile with the handheld controls. I loved watching Batman and Robin on TV, and I can still smell the food my mom would cook up for us every evening as we watched the show. When I think of her cooking, I think of fried potatoes with corn bread, and vegetables from the garden for Dad and fried chicken, mashed potatoes, and coleslaw for us girls.

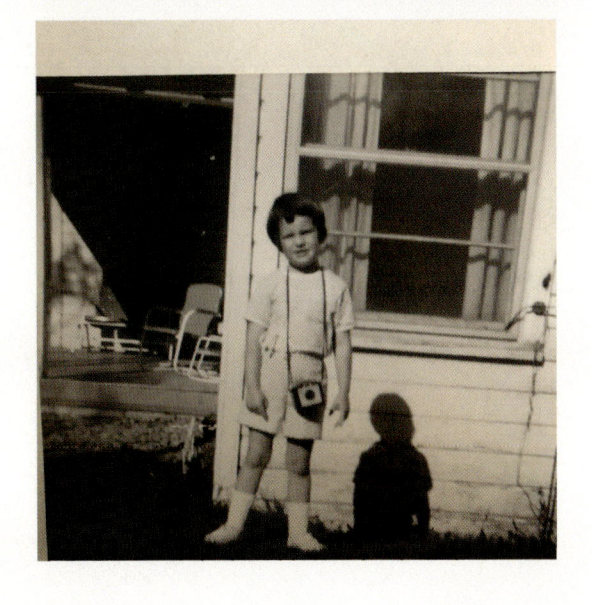

Fourth of July

The Fourth of July is one of our favorite gatherings for friends and family. It is a great chance to serve my loved ones a delicious meal. What's better than a grilled hamburger or hotdog with cold cucumber, tomato, and onion salad? Traditional macaroni and pasta salads aren't too bad either. In Olive Hill, where we live, the Fourth of July is a two-week celebration in honor of the storyteller singer Tom T Hall who was born and raised in our little town in eastern Kentucky. The celebration is complete with beauty pageants, horse shows, concerts in the street, fireworks and more! When the girls were small, we used to celebrate every Fourth of July at my mom's house near town. For the last thirteen years, we have traveled instead to our beach house in Florida. For a recent Fourth of July at the beach, we had a low country boil. It was so much fun to serve! Our son-in-law Mark was the chef, and he used shrimp, red potatoes, corn on the cob, and crawdad tails. Not only was this meal beautifully displayed along the middle of the table, but it was tasty too! The farm fresh vegetables and seafood purchased from a local fish market made the meal extra special. Our grandson Wells and I made cupcakes and fresh Blackberry cobbler, decorated with tiny American flags. With a couple requests for my fresh-squeezed lemonade, I made two pitchers - one sweet and one unsweet to satisfy the crowd.

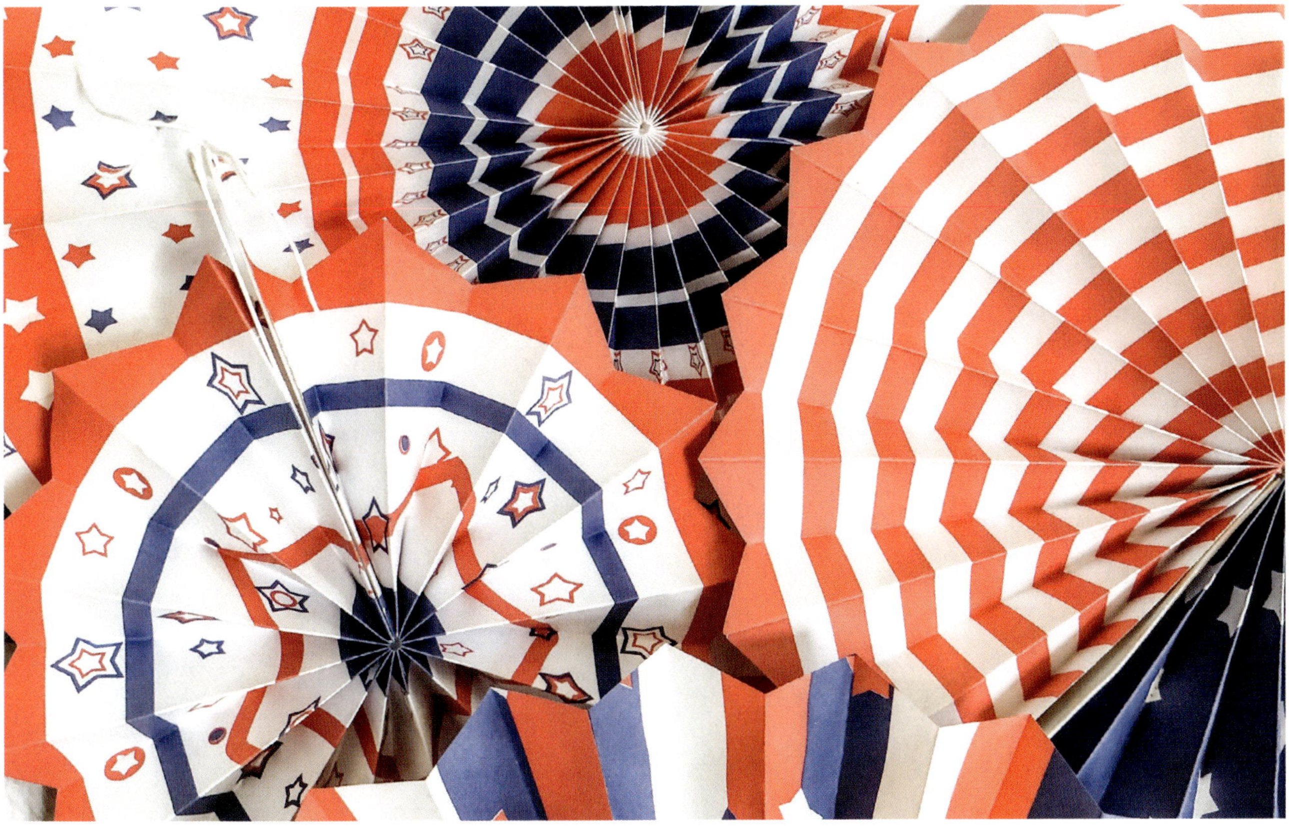

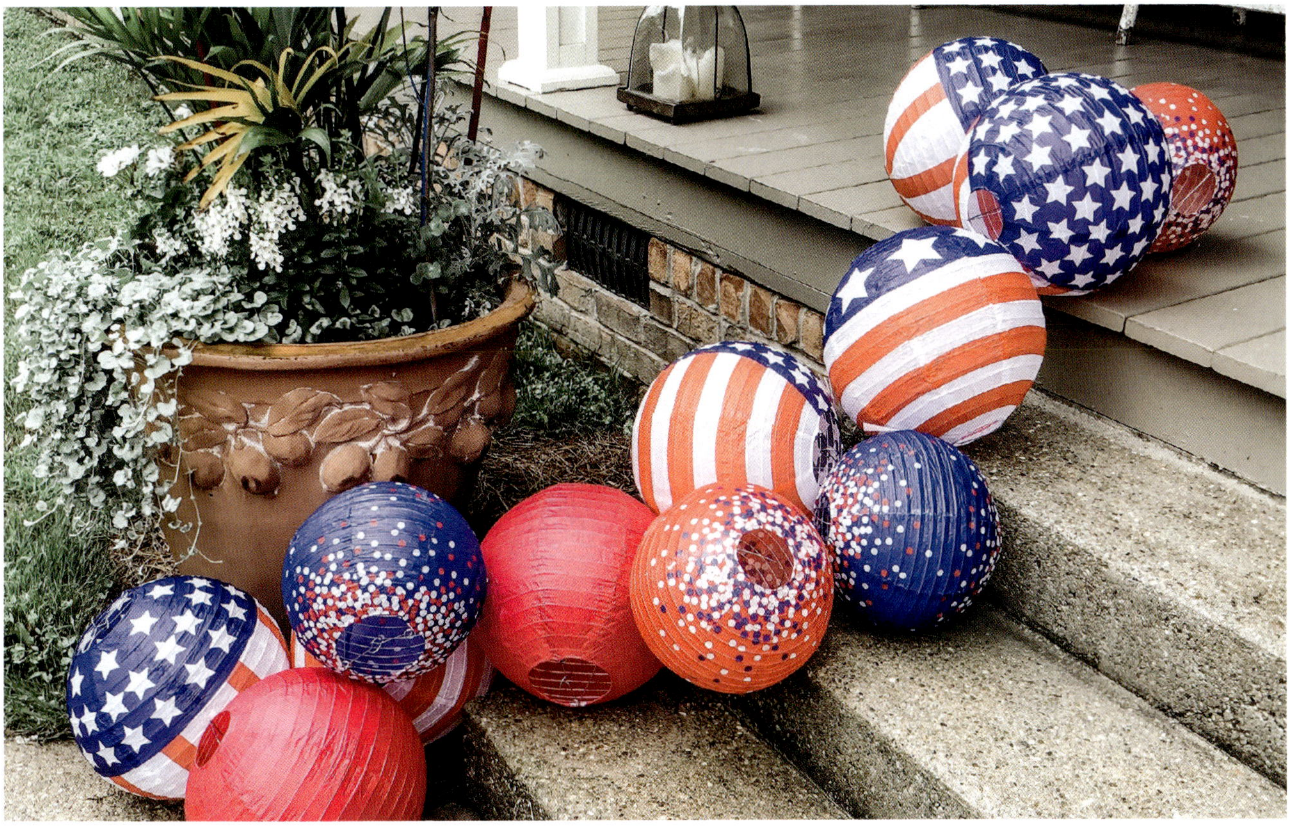

The Fourth of July may be one of the easiest holidays to decorate. You will need flags, flags, and more flags! Tablecloths made from yards of denim make a beautiful table cover. White dishes add a fresh, clean appearance and are a great canvas for colorful, fresh, summer dishes. I have been collecting vintage sand pails for years, and I love to use them as centerpieces for a summertime party.   Nothing says summer better than sand buckets and beach shovels!

Vinegar Salad

1 1/2 cups vinegar

2 cups water

1 cup sugar

1 English cucumber (peeled and sliced)

1 large tomato (slice into small wedges)

1 medium sweet onion (sliced in small rings) you can add more sugar if you prefer

Mix vinegar, water, and sugar together until sugar is dissolved. Add sliced cucumbers, tomatoes, and onions to vinegar mixture. Refrigerate for two hours.

Decorative Fireworks Craft

- Use one red, one white, and one blue foam pool noodle.
- Use a saw to cut the noodles into three different sizes. I used 15.5", 12.5", and 8.5" for a decoration that sits on my mantel. Adjust the height of the firecracker to suit its place.
- Use 12x12" patriotic scrapbook paper to cover the cut noodles. You can also use electrical tape to decorate the noodles.
- After wrapping the firecracker, measure the diameter of each noodle with a piece of paper, and cut out two circles to glue over each end.
- Use firecracker food picks to stick in the top of each firecracker to complete the look. So festive!

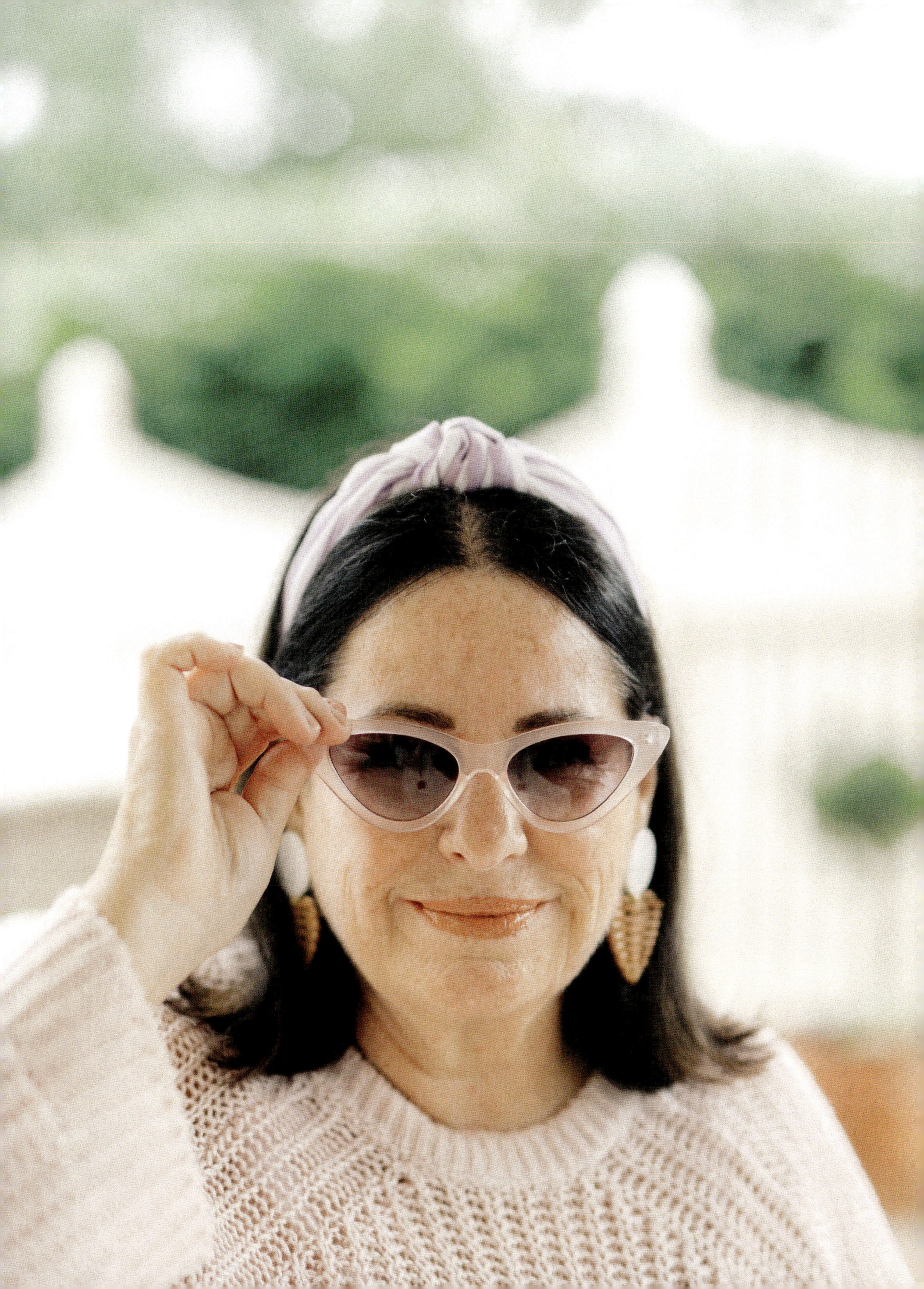

Southern Peach Cobbler

Ingredients

1 stick of real butter

1 ½ cup of self-rising flour

1 ½ cup of sugar

12oz can of Carnation Evaporated Milk

29 oz can of peaches with syrup

Instructions

Spray baking dish with Pam spray. Melt butter in baking dish in 350-degree oven. Mix together flour, sugar and milk. Pour into baking dish. Add can of peaches and syrup last. (I cut my peaches into smaller pieces before I add them to the recipe.) Bake for 50-55 minutes. Serve warm with vanilla ice-cream.

Cultivate your outdoor space and make it an extension of your living area. We brought the French Riviera to our outdoor space by using bright stripes, fresh fruit and flowers.

Autumn's Chill Marches In

I love beautiful colors and crisp evenings of autumn. As the weather grows colder, it sparks in me a desire to make my home warm and welcoming for anyone who cares to stop by. The next holiday has been a favorite of mine since my niece, nephew, and I were small. [my sister was almost twenty years older than me, so her children and I were close in age]. Trick or treating brought so much excitement to our little neighborhood. The most favorite treat I ever received was from a lady who sold Avon for a living. She would pass out her small samples of lipstick which were in small gold tubes about one inch long to all us girls, and candy for the boys.

Halloween

One of the best things about fall is hosting a Spook-tacular Halloween Porch Party!

As the little ghouls and goblins parade through your neighborhood, have special treats ready to greet them at your haunted porch party. Display favorite treats for all to enjoy, even the adults!

Spooky Candle Display

Using food graters with candles behind them makes a scary entrance to any home.

I love making caramel popcorn balls and witch hat sandwiches for the little goblins. Don't forget to serve hot apple cider for the adults to enjoy as well. Here are my recipes for the popcorn balls, which hat sandwiches, and the apple cider.

Caramel Popcorn Balls

1 cup butter
1 cup light corn syrup
2 cups packed light brown sugar
1/2 cup granulated sugar
1 14 oz sweetened condensed milk
1 Tbsp vanilla
8-12 cups popped popcorn (less will be messier, and gooier).
I usually double this recipe because it makes only 8 large balls

1. Bring the butter, syrup, and sugars to a boil, let bubble over medium heat until it gets to soft ball stage

2. Add the sweetened condensed milk, and vanilla and boil approximately one more minute. Let it cool a little so it doesn't shrink the popcorn.

3. Pour over the popcorn and stir

4. Spread popcorn out on a nonstick surface to cool

5. Spray your hands with cooking spray and start forming the balls

6. Allow shaped balls to cool so they will hold their shape

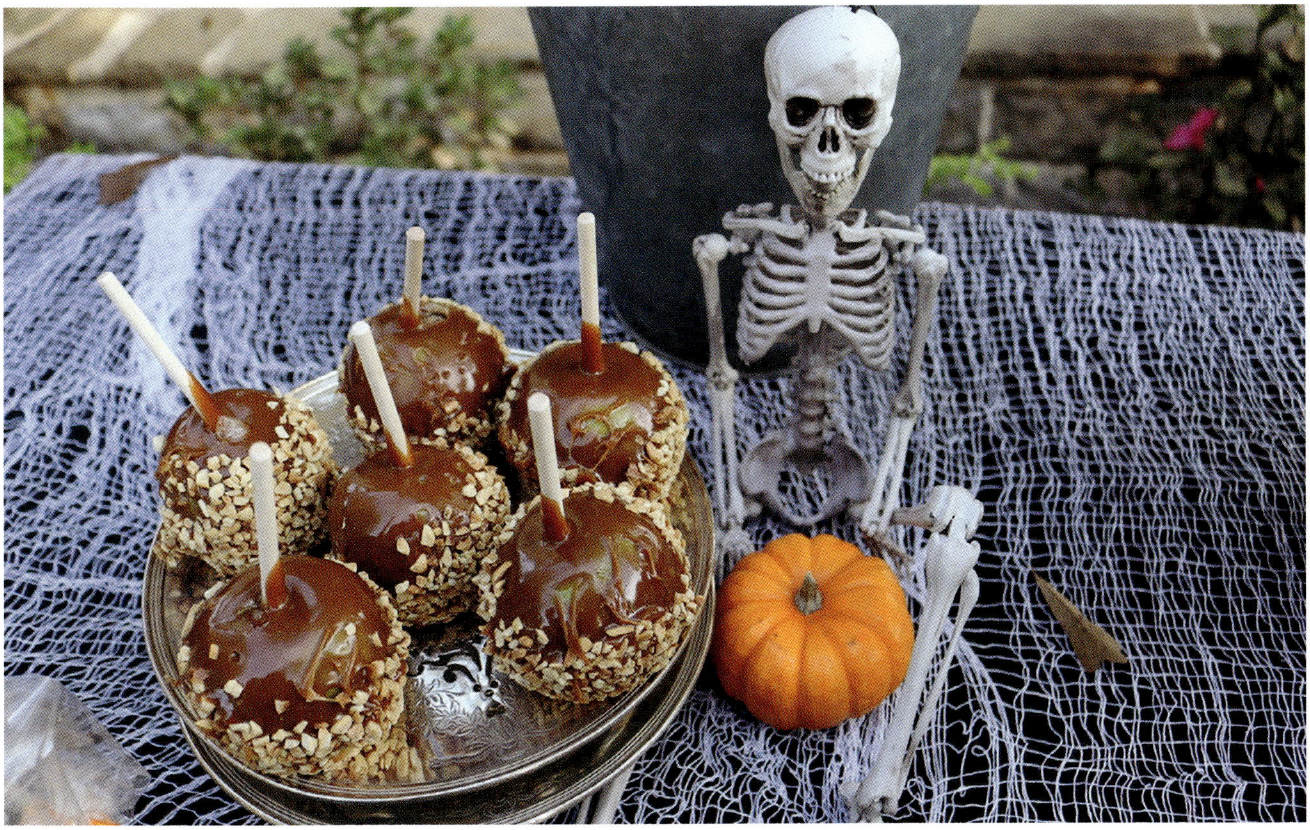

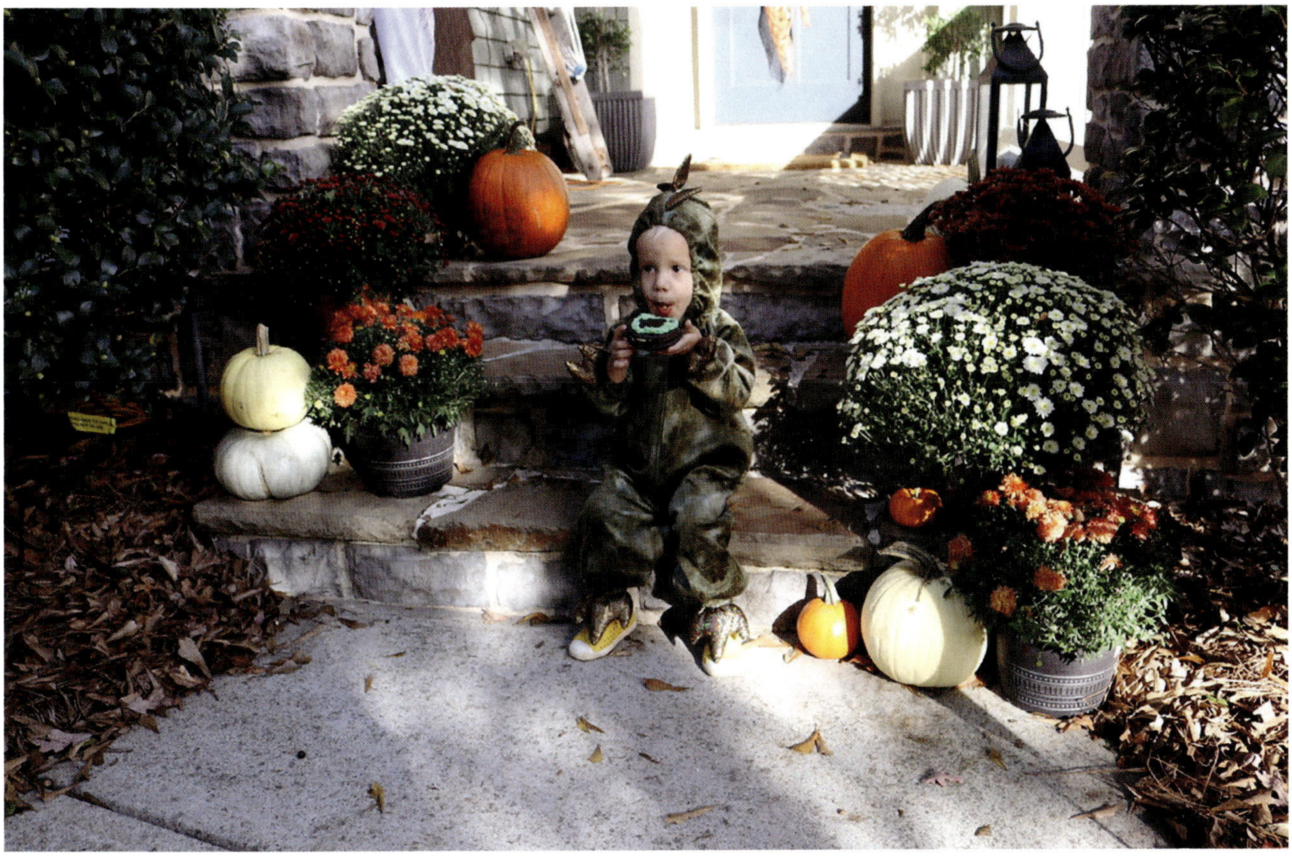

Witch Hat Moon Pie Sandwich

- 2 boxes of chocolate sugar ice cream cones
- 2 cans of Betty Crocker green icing with tips to use as glue
- 24 or less chocolate covered moon pies

Set the cones in the center of the moon pie and glue in place with the green icing.
Ta Da! You have one of the cutest and simplest Halloween treats for your little goblins.

Warm Apple Cider

- 1 box of apple cider mulling spice
- 1-gallon real apple cider

Mix well over medium heat until mixture with spices and sugar has dissolved.

Serve warm.

You can also add bourbon for some extra fun!

Thanksgiving

In late fall I rely on mother nature to supply me with the inspiration I need to decorate our home for the holidays. Nothing sets the tone better for Thanksgiving than the time-honored pumpkin. I have been using the Ghostly White variety for an elegant pumpkin display for years. Because of their unusual color, they add interest to table centerpieces, vignettes, and porch decor alike. Pretty silver candlesticks and trays look great with these beauties. Candlesticks also serve to add height without overpowering the table. If you want to add a hint of color, you can incorporate seasonal berries, flowers, and even branches from trees in your yard. Remember anything goes!

The Most Wonderful Time of the Year

In our home, there is no holiday more joyous than Christmas. The halls of our house are decked in holiday flair that reflects our eclectic style and love of the holidays. My main goal for the Christmas celebration is to create the general feeling of warmth and joy. Every year during the holiday season our family gathers around our dining room table to make Christmas ornaments to share with family and friends. We also make chocolate-covered cherries, peanut butter balls, rock cinnamon candy, and we have decorated our very own gingerbread houses in the past.

We use our ornaments and decorations year after year, giving our home a well-worn and nostalgic feel. Our Christmas tree stands proud laden with forty years of ornaments we have collected and received as gifts. Each ornament invites a little spark of joy as it is unwrapped and hung on the tree.

When changing your vignettes around the house for the holidays, shop in your own home! Add and subtract items until each vignette feels balanced and beautiful. In our home, fresh greenery is key. There's nothing that says Christmas better than the aroma of live trees, wreaths, and garlands.

Each year, we take a trip to the woods to find holly and mistletoe. The smell of being in nature and out in the fresh air sets the tone for our Christmas celebration. Inside our home, I dry orange slices to be used in a cranberry, orange, and popcorn garland for the tree. The smell of the oranges always takes me back to the cozy house where I grew up at Christmas time. My parents always had a big basket of fruit and nuts dead center of the kitchen table for us to enjoy during the holidays. Who doesn't love the smell of Christmas? We add slices of oranges and lemons with allspice and lots of cinnamon to a pan of water placed on top of the stove. As the mixture simmers, it releases the most wonderful Christmas aroma.

83

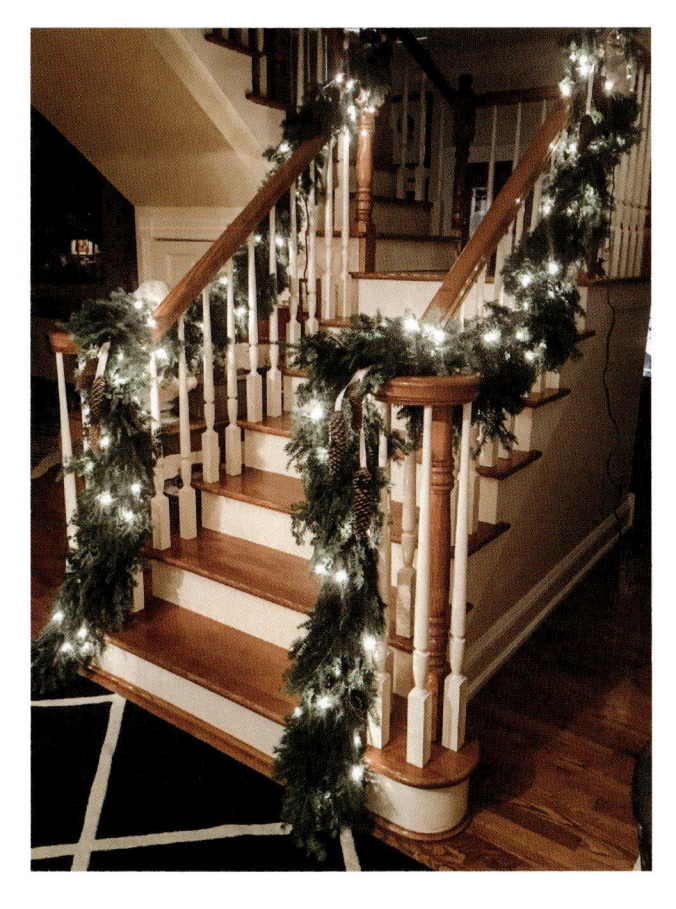

Christmas Potpourri

One large orange sliced
One lemon sliced
1 tablespoon allspice
2 tablespoon cinnamon

Combine ingredients with pot of water and boil.

The most wonderful time of the year

Baking cakes and making candy are great traditions for all, especially when you have young ones to help. Cooking together in the kitchen is a fantastic way to make memories that you will all cherish.

In our home on Christmas, the oldest adult (preferably a grandparent) or one of the children read the story of Christmas from the Bible. We sing Christmas carols, play games, and enjoy lots of sweets while taking in the beauty of our family around us. Santa comes on Christmas Eve, and on Christmas morning we open the gifts that he left the night before.

My husband, Willie, and I cook a large Christmas breakfast for all to enjoy after the gifts have been opened. Why do we love this magical time of year so much, and look forward to it all year long? Because Christmas is about togetherness, showing love to strangers or someone in need, celebrating our children, and remembering what matters. The holiday season is definitely the time of year that many of us feel like giving back. Donations in America increase about forty-two percent in November and December.

Pink Christmas

Who remembers the retro pink of the 1960's? I have always wanted to use these colors at Christmas time and this year, I went for it. I used a more muted version of these hues and embellished with fresh greenery to fill the house with the smell of pine. See what you think!

88

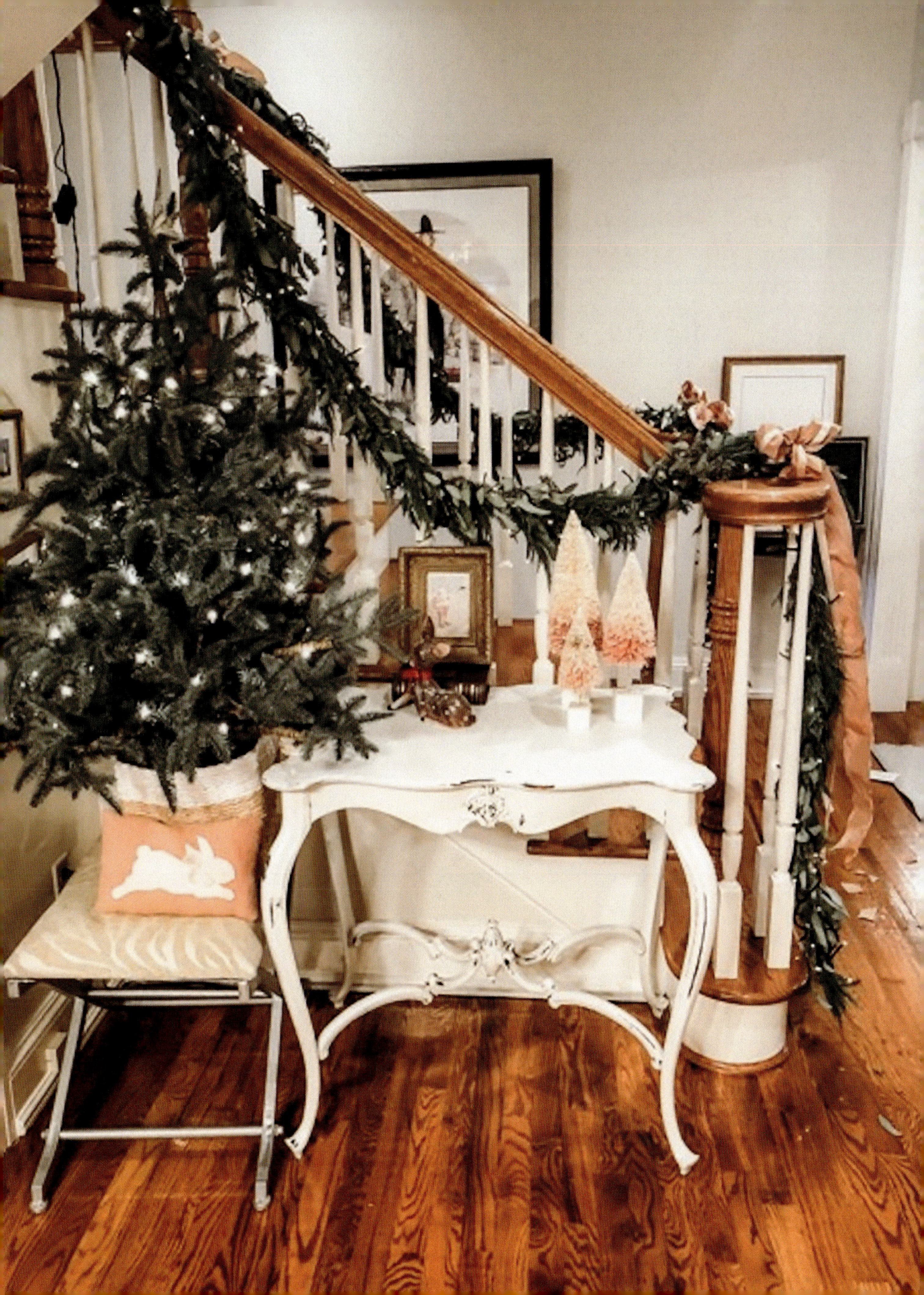

PARTIES THROUGHOUT THE YEAR

Who doesn't love a party? I love throwing parties while opening my home and making others feel welcome and cared for when they visit.

Baby Showers

When our youngest daughter Holli, and her husband, Mark, told us they were expecting our grandson Wells, I started planning the baby shower the very next day. Although they live in Atlanta, they wanted to host the party in Kentucky for family and friends. Mark's parents hosted a beautiful shower for the new parents to be in Atlanta also. A baby shower can be a simple affair, or you can go all out. Anyone who knows me knows I go overboard for my children, so we had a gorgeous outdoor shower by the pool. We were blessed with the most beautiful day we could have asked for. I'm not a big fan of games at a shower, so we didn't have organized activities. Our guests did, however, each leave with door prizes and parting gifts. On Holli's request, we kept the guest list to twenty, which was a perfect number. With too many people it's difficult for the host to visit with each guest and to thank them properly. For the baby shower, we enjoyed inviting guests who made an impression on Holli growing up and the people who loves her the most. One of Holli's friends is a professional photographer, and it was such a treat to have someone memorializing the day.

92

Party and Shower Planning Tips

- Make a list of everyone you want to come. Try to invite guests who have something in common. This will help the conversation run more smoothly. As the host, it will be your job to engage every guest and keep the party exciting.

- Check with the people you want to invite to make sure that the date works well for most. Ask for RSVPs! As a side note, if you are invited to a party, please please please RSVP immediately! The host is going to go to a lot of trouble to prepare their home. If you can't make the party, let the host know as soon as possible if you will be attending or not. Don't be a NSNN (No Show, No Notice)!

- Once you start receiving RSVPs, consider what kind of food you will serve. Although planning in advance is great, don't make the mistake of prepping too far in advance. Buy any ingredients for food the day before the party for maximum freshness. If the party is on a Saturday night, give yourself Friday to prepare. Taking as much time as you need to prepare is a good way to reduce anxiety. Then, on Saturday morning, you can drink your coffee (or morning beverage of choice), and take your time setting the table, putting finishing touches on decorations, and completing any last-minute food assembly that can't be done the day before. Get a few moments of rest before you begin preparing the meal.

- As your guests start arriving, make sure everyone has a drink in their hand. My husband usually takes on this duty, and he has a special gift for making our guests feel welcome and comfortable. I always offer a non-alcoholic cocktail with a festive garnish alongside the spiked beverages, so everyone feels special.

- It's a good idea to have a charcuterie board with appetizers for guests to munch on as they arrive. We serve cheese and crackers with olives and pickles to get the party started as conversation warms up. I often serve red and white wine with board of food.

- Depending on the occasion, serve the meal accordingly. For a basketball party, a buffet style works well. Every now and then, I like to set a pretty table and serve dinner that way.

Fresh vegetables for your party are key. Parties in Spring Summer or Fall require you to have the freshest vegetables available. These can be grown outside in a garden or if you are short on space raised beds are a compact way to have a variety of vegetables close at hand. Local farmer's markets are a great place to visit also to acquire fresh fruits and vegetables. My husband has built raised beds from recycled lumber and placed them in different areas of our yard. We love having fresh veggies all spring, summer and even in the fall season of the year. One of our favorites are snow peas that make a beautiful green presentation early in the season. After a cold winter of snow and ice it's always nice to see the first sprouts of green popping through the earth. Lettuce and onions are a favorite, but spinach, radishes, and other greens grow well in these small spaces too. Tomatoes work well but must be spaced eighteen to twenty-four inches apart. In our boxes we have room for four tomato plants in each box. This method of gardening is simple yet easily accessible and maintained.

Jack's Peter Rabbit Birthday Party

When our Grandson Jack turned one year old, his birthday party that we hosted was a favorite. We spent days working to come up with a theme for Jack's birthday party, then one day he toddled down to the raised vegetable garden in his back yard and picked a small green tomato from the vine. Both Jack and his brother Wells love helping in the garden and learning about harvesting fruits and vegetables. This gave us the idea to use the story of Peter Rabbit's Garden as a theme for the party. It just so happens that Mark and Holli (Jack's parents) have the perfect back yard with two large garden gates which fit nicely with the theme.

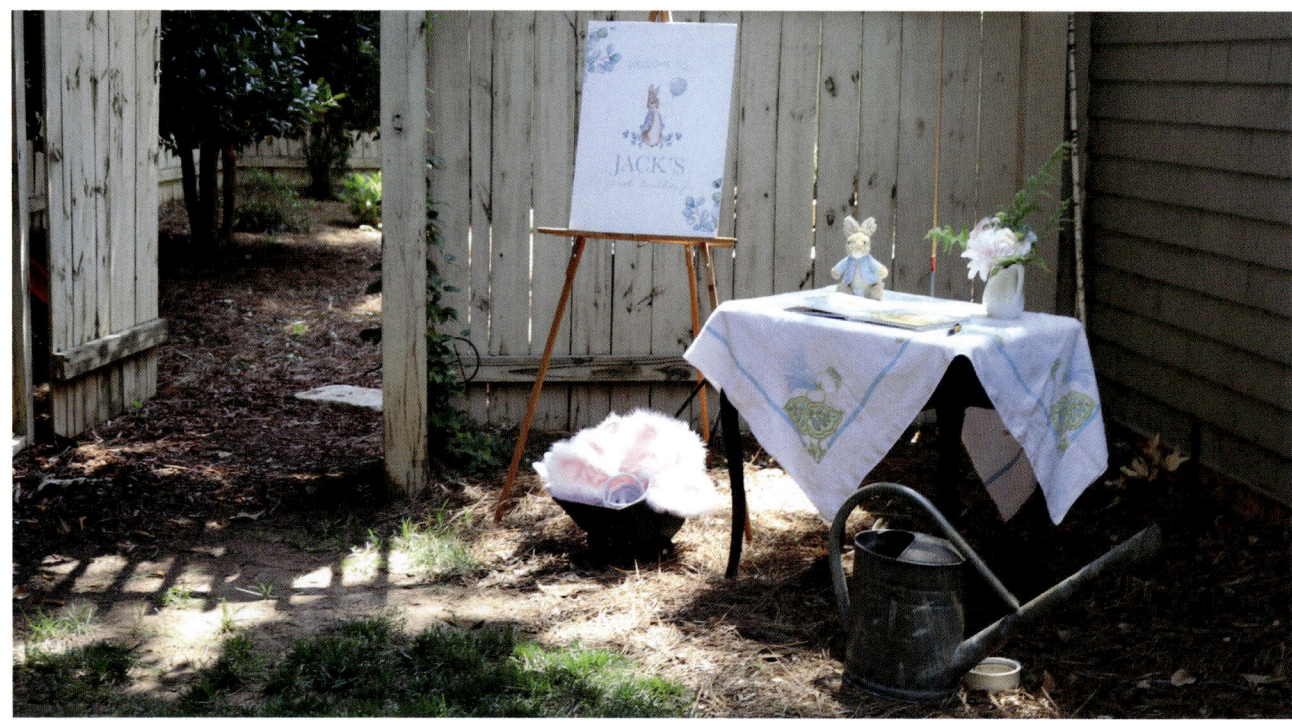

97

When setting up for the party, we started by moving the family dining room table and chairs to the center of the backyard. I covered it with a fun striped blue and white fabric which I had found through an on-line store. We then placed a hand painted Peter Rabbit sign outside the gate to mark the entrance to the party. Handmade signs led the guests through the garden gate to the world of Peter Rabbit and ending at Mr. McGregor's garden.

I truly enjoyed gathering and creating the props, tables, garden tools, watering cans, wooden crates, cake stand, utensils, table clothes and partyware for the occasion. All are items you can collect over time and I can promise you will pull them out over and over for your own celebrations.

Try to use fresh flowers if available as they add a special touch to any party. I was able to find green and purple cabbage and carrots with the green tops still attached at the local grocery store which created the perfect center piece for our theme.

We sat up a designated photo area with a backdrop of Peter Rabbit against the fence from two large wooden crates put together for the children to sit on for photos.

Signs were used in Mr. McGregor's garden with Peter's little blue jacket. I used a clothesline where Peter's brother, Cottontail's, sweater and shoes were hung to dry. I pulled out a doll table and chairs that belonged to our daughters when they were young for Flopsy's tea party with friends under the shade of a tree in the yard. I hung a small chandelier over the little table which added enjoyment for the little girls in attendance.

A copy of the Story of Peter Rabbit served as the guest book for those who came to sign and to share messages for Jack to read and enjoy when he is older.

The food served was simple but delicious and seemed enjoyable to even the picky eaters who attended.

Vegetable pizza
Vegetable and fruit snacks for the children
Cheese spread with crackers
Chicken salad sandwiches
Cucumber sandwiches
Fresh vegetables and dip
Carrot cupcakes
Fruit pies

Last but certainly not least, we were able to find a local farmer who was willing to bring some animals from his farm and create a small petting zoo in the back yard. He brought small wooden fencing to contain the ducks, chickens, pot belly pig, sheep, goats and rabbits.

This was the perfect ending to the perfect day.

Thankfully mother nature cooperated and gave us beautiful weather for this special event.

Each child received an orange bubble blower with a green ribbon attached to take home and enjoy.

Credits
Hand painted Peter Rabbit sign- Christy Brown
Cottontails sweater and shoes-Cole Brown
Flopsy's table and chairs-Jack's Mother Holli and Aunt Jessi
Chandelier other props and party signs-Mam and Pops
Hoe and rake-Wells
Wooden crates-Hobby lobby
Dining table and chairs-Mommy and Daddy
Veggie and Cucumber Sandwiches- Nana and Papa Jim
Pies and Carrot cupcakes- Southern Baked Pie Company
Farm animals- Mr. McGregor
Red Tractor- Donated by John Sewell

To Our Wonderful Jack Eddie

We adore everything about you. Your sweet personality, contagious smile and oh THOSE DIMPLES!! You captured our hearts the first time we held you. This birthday party celebrates your first year of life and we will continue to celebrate you for the rest of our days.

Wedding Reception

A wedding reception is a party held after the completion of a marriage ceremony. It is held usually as hospitality for those who have attended the wedding, hence the name reception: the couple receives society, in the form of family and friends, for the first time as a married couple.

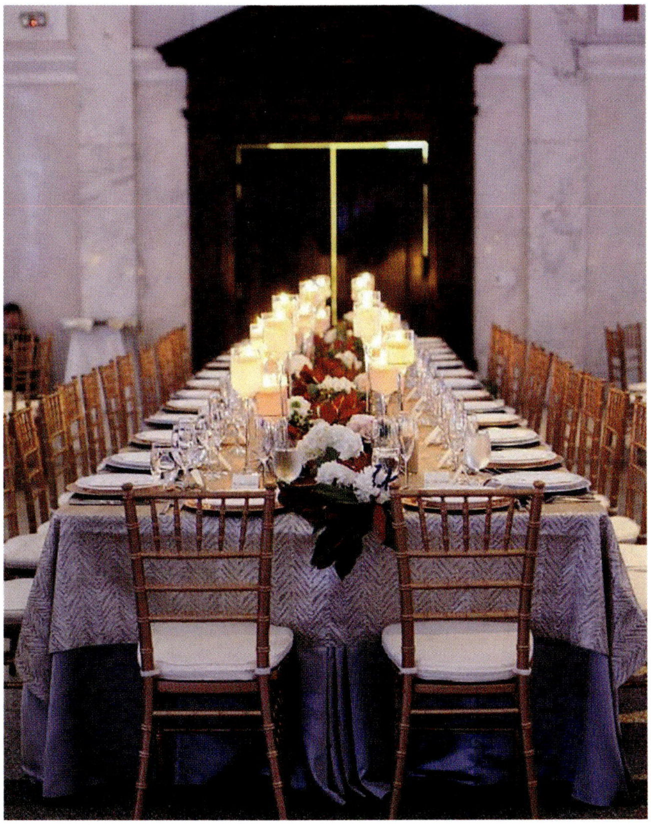

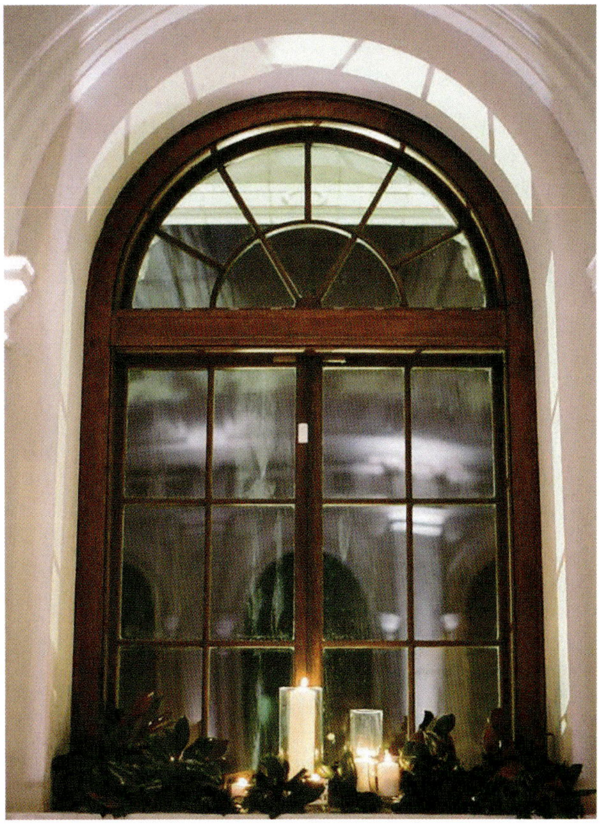

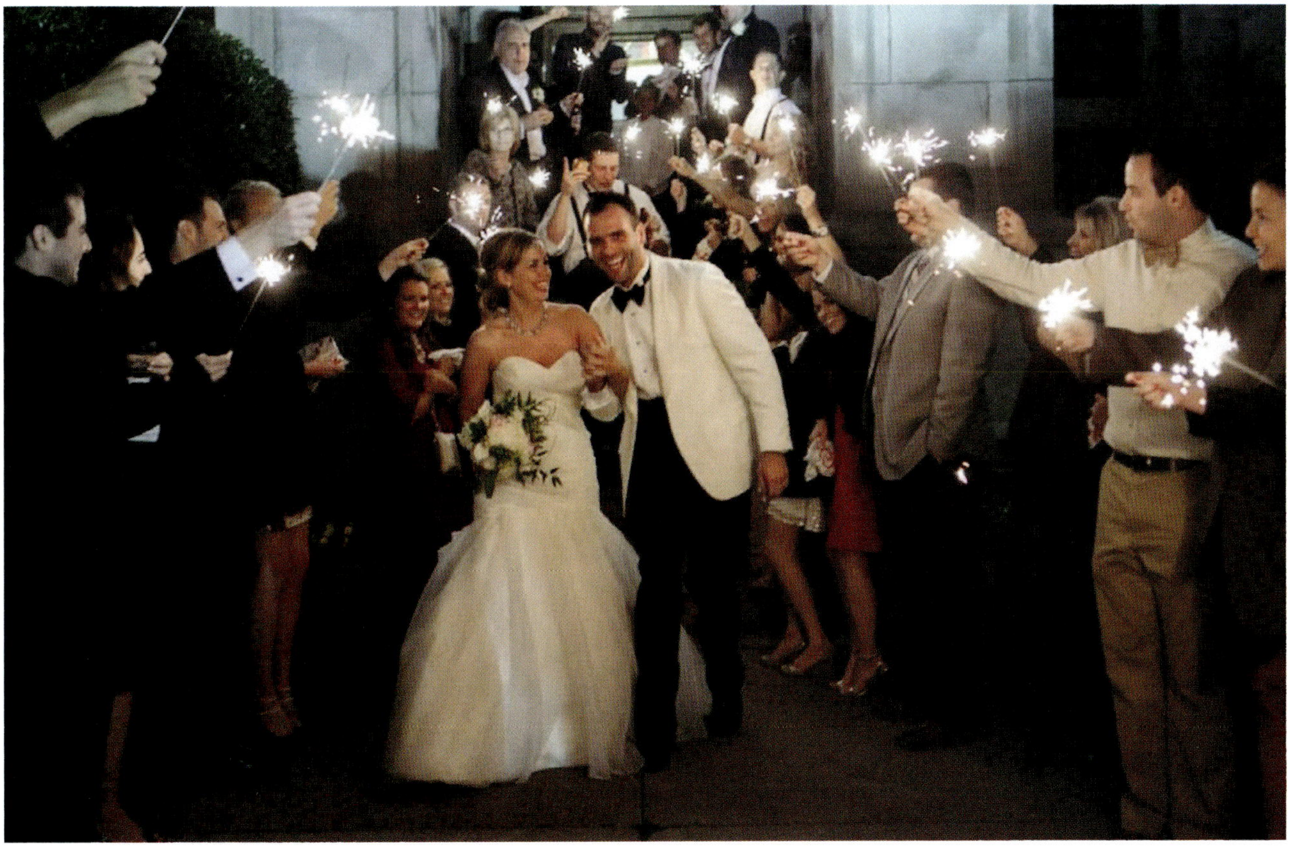

In closing...

I love making my home pretty while challenging myself to make it functional. We in the south strive for hospitality and charm, while making visitors and family alike to feel welcome, comfortable, and at home.

Being raised in a small town with great people and strong women around me has made me the person I am today. I want everyone to embrace their beautiful style, while living with what you love. Visit the beach as often as you can, curl up in a beautiful quilt, and make life cozy.

Remember to incorporate the old and the new, be humble but be GRAND with your style. Stay organized and remember less is more. Be creative, while doing things that excites you. Cherish heirlooms, and have a variety of vignettes throughout your home. Do some porch sittin'. Keep your rooms fresh. Sit with your face to the sun, and your back to the wind. Go crazy with the holidays, but hold on to traditions. Take a trip to clear your mind, and another to nourish the soul. Do all these things for the people you love the most, your family.

Kimberly

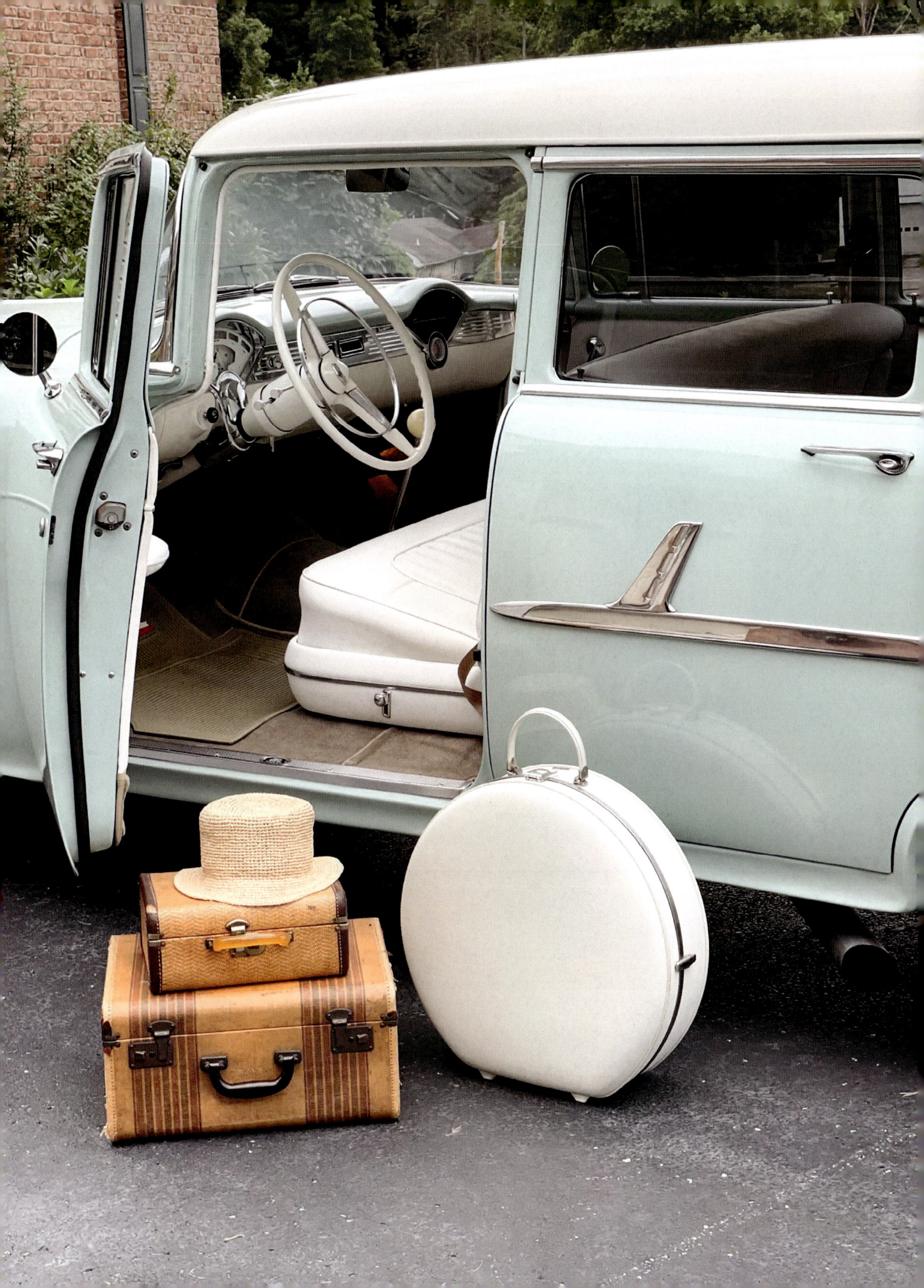

Acknowledgements

Jessi, you were the first to believe that I could put pen to paper and make sense of it. Thank you for all the many hours of hard work in setting up this entire book. I love you for that, believing in your Mama, and at times giving me the push I needed to complete the book. This story would not have come together if not for you. The time we spent together on this book will always hold a special place in my heart.

Steffen, thank you for your understanding and patience while Jessi spent hours helping me with this project.

Holli, thank you for reading my draft and gently critiquing my story. You are my inspiration in life. I pray daily to be more like you. You are the very definition of grace. You and Mark make life look easy.

Mark, thank you for patiently answering all my questions and giving me countless tips on my Instagram postings. The photos and text messages that come almost daily are what makes living so far apart bearable for Willie and I.

Willie, thanks for always supporting and encouraging me through every step of this project. You have sit for hours listening to me read and reread these pages out loud. Many times we have worked on my book while driving to and from Atlanta for seven or eight hours at a time. I'm so fortunate to share this life with you. You are my rock and the best husband, father and now Poppy. I can hardly wait for our next adventure to come.

To my sister Toni, thank you for being such a cheerleader in my life and convincing me that all things are possible with hard work. You were the best. I miss you so much.

Christy, thank you for the support you have always given me. It is such a blessing that we live close enough to share our lives and the raising of our families and grandchildren. Thanks for all the last-minute art projects that you somehow find the time to help me with. Jack's Peter Rabbit birthday party would not have been the same without your help. Your talent has no boundaries.

My nephew Rick, you were born with the talent of design, and I learned from you. Miss you every day.

Friends, thanks be to you for inspirations, your prayers and always making time to go "junking," work out at the gym or an out-of-town shopping trip just so we could visit and spend the day together. You are all the best and I love you for our many years of friendship.

To the boys who have made me a grandmother. You fill my life with never ending joy. I am so excited that you will have this book which has captured so many moments in your young lives. I hope you know how much I enjoy bringing ideas to life to make your celebrations so special.

Mrs. Dehart and Miss Ross - Thanks to these two strong women who instilled in me at an early age, the strength and the tools I would need to navigate life. You both are the epitome of what a teacher should be.

My Mom and Dad, you were the best parents my sisters and I could have asked for. Hard working parents who lived for their children. I love and miss you more than I could ever put into words.

Thanks be to God for giving me the drive for entertaining, the love for decorating. I pray that this book will bring enjoyment and appreciation for life's moments and memories spent with loved ones in all the beautiful seasons of the year. I hope it brings glory to your name.